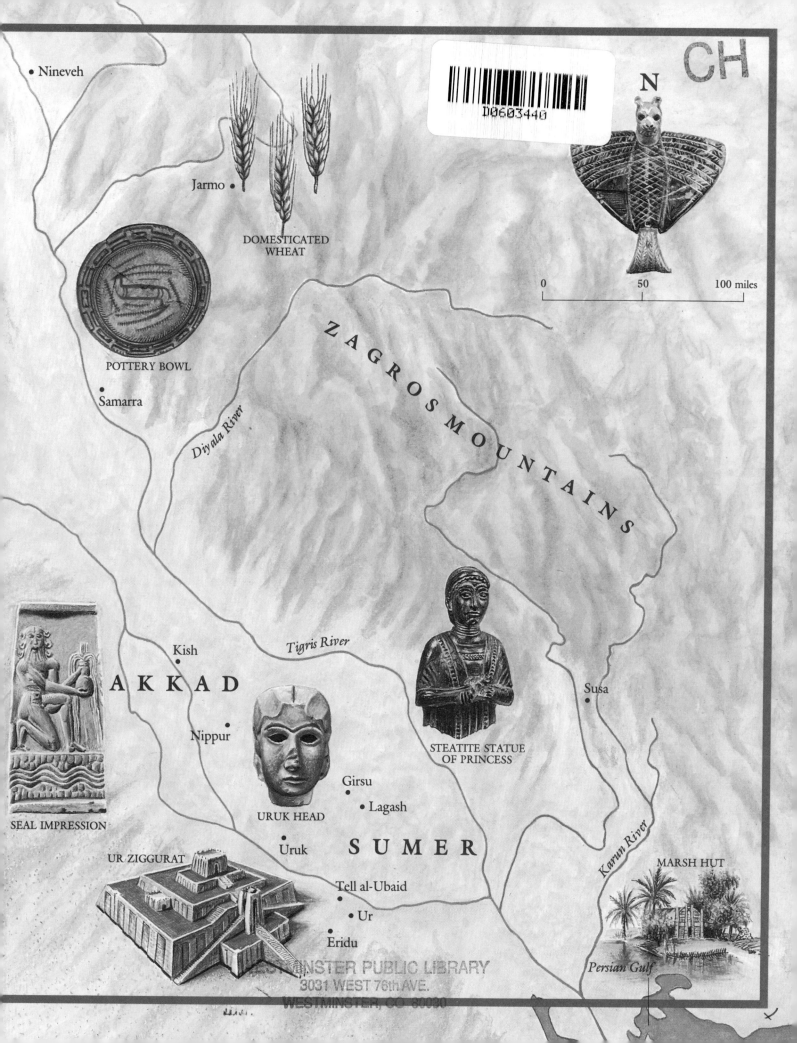

• Nineveh

Jarmo •

DOMESTICATED
WHEAT

POTTERY BOWL

• Samarra

Diyala River

Z A G R O S   M O U N T A I N S

N

CH

0   50   100 miles

Kish
•

A K K A D

Nippur
•

Tigris River

SEAL IMPRESSION

Susa
•

STEATITE STATUE
OF PRINCESS

Girsu
•

• Lagash

URUK HEAD

Uruk
•

S U M E R

Karun River

MARSH HUT

UR ZIGGURAT

Tell al-Ubaid
•

• Ur

Eridu
•

Persian Gulf

SUMER:
CITIES OF
EDEN

TIME-LIFE BOOKS

EDITOR-IN-CHIEF: Thomas H. Flaherty
Director of Editorial Resources: Elise D. Ritter-Clough
Executive Art Director: Ellen Robling
Director of Photography and Research: John Conrad Weiser
Editorial Board: Dale M. Brown, Janet Cave, Roberta Conlan, Robert Doyle, Laura Foreman, Jim Hicks, Rita Thievon Mullin, Henry Woodhead
Assistant Director of Editorial Resources: Norma E. Shaw

PRESIDENT: John D. Hall

Vice President and Director of Marketing: Nancy K. Jones
Editorial Director: Russell B. Adams, Jr.
Director of Production Services: Robert N. Carr
Production Manager: Prudence G. Harris
Director of Technology: Eileen Bradley
Supervisor of Quality Control: James King

Editorial Operations
Production: Celia Beattie
Library: Louise D. Forstall
Computer Composition: Deborah G. Tait (Manager), Monika D. Thayer, Janet Barnes Syring, Lillian Daniels
Interactive Media Specialist: Patti H. Cass

Time-Life Books is a division of Time Life Incorporated

PRESIDENT AND CEO: John M. Fahey, Jr.

**Library of Congress
Cataloging in Publication Data**
Sumer: cities of Eden / by the editors of Time-Life Books.
    p. cm.—(Lost civilizations)
Includes bibliographical references and index.
ISBN 0-8094-9887-1 (trade)
ISBN 0-8094-9888-X (lib. bdg.)
    1. Babylonia—Civilization.
    2. Cities, Ancient—Iraq—Babylonia.
I. Time-Life Books. II. Series.
DS69.5.S78   1993
935—dc20   92-38367

LOST CIVILIZATIONS

SERIES EDITOR: Dale M. Brown
Administrative Editor: Philip Brandt George

Editorial staff for: *Sumer: Cities of Eden*
Art Director: Susan K. White
Picture Editor: Kristin Baker Hanneman
Text Editor: James Michael Lynch
Writers: Denise Dersin, Charles J. Hagner, Darcie Conner Johnston
Associate Editor/Research: Jacqueline L. Shaffer
Assistant Editor/Research: Katherine L. Griffin
Assistant Art Director: Bill McKenney
Senior Copyeditor: Jarelle S. Stein
Picture Coordinator: David A. Herod
Editorial Assistant: Patricia D. Whiteford

Special Contributors: Tony Allan, Windsor Chorlton, Lydia Preston Hicks, Alan J. Lothian, Valerie Moolman, David S. Thomson, Terry J. White (text); Vilasini Balakrishnan, Patti H. Cass, Margaret McKinnon Gardner, Ann-Louise Gates, Gail Prensky (research); Roy Nanovic (index)

Correspondents: Elisabeth Kraemer-Singh (Bonn), Christine Hinze (London), Christina Lieberman (New York), Maria Vincenza Aloisi (Paris), Ann Natanson (Rome). Valuable assistance was also provided by: Judy Aspinall (London); Corky Bastlund (Copenhagen); Elizabeth Brown, Katheryn White (New York); Ann Wise (Rome); Dick Berry (Tokyo).

The Consultants:
James A. Armstrong teaches at the University of Chicago, where he is a research associate at the Oriental Institute. He has worked extensively on archaeological excavations in Iraq, including those at the prominent Sumerian site of Nippur. As a Fulbright scholar in Iraq, he directed the first season of excavations at Tell al-Deylam in 1989-1990, but the project had to be canceled due to the events leading up to the Persian Gulf War.

Richard L. Zettler, a professor of anthropology at the University of Pennsylvania and assistant curator at the University Museum, has lectured and written about ancient Mesopotamia for many years. In addition, since 1974 he has served as site supervisor, assistant director, or codirector of several excavations in Syria and Iraq.

Juris Zarins has nearly 20 years experience in the field of Near Eastern archaeology. He has served as archaeological advisor to the Ministry of Education of the Kingdom of Saudi Arabia, participated in and directed a number of field surveys and excavations, and has written numerous articles on his finds. He now teaches in the Department of Sociology and Anthropology at Southwest Missouri State University.

SUMER: CITIES OF EDEN

By the Editors of Time-Life Books

TIME-LIFE BOOKS, ALEXANDRIA, VIRGINIA

CONTENTS

Silhouetted by the rising sun, a solitary boat plies a palm-lined expanse of the lower Tigris River in present-day Iraq. The immemorial scene recalls the setting of Sumer, the world's first civilization, which arose on the arid alluvial plain between the Tigris and the Euphrates rivers, nurtured by their life-giving waters.

HISTORY'S FORGOTTEN PEOPLE

One of the first works of Sumerian art ever found, this statuette was unearthed by diplomat turned archaeologist Ernest de Sarzec during his 1880 dig at Telloh—ancient Girsu. The figure probably portrays a princess of Lagash, the city-state to which Girsu belonged.

The French diplomat Ernest de Sarzec had time on his hands. In 1877 he was serving as vice-consul in the port of Basra, a hot, sleepy outpost of the Ottoman Empire located at the head of the Persian Gulf in what is today's Iraq. The duties of his job were undemanding, for few French travelers or traders passed that way, and there was little for him to do except go riding, shoot game birds, or hunt wild boar in the scrubby desert surrounding the town. He soon tired of these activities and sought something more rewarding to occupy his long leisure hours.

The region of Mesopotamia—a term used to describe the land between the rivers Tigris and Euphrates, near whose confluence the port of Basra lies—was rich in history. Babylonia and Assyria, cited often in the Old Testament, were familiar throughout the Western world, though few scholars or laypersons had the opportunity to visit the isolated area. Sarzec, who had whetted his appetite for ancient cultures during previous assignments in Egypt and Ethiopia, was eager to explore the remains of Mesopotamia's bygone civilizations.

By chance, a director of the French Post Office, who was conducting an inspection tour of telegraph lines, came across an interesting site called Telloh, 155 miles southeast of Baghdad, and informed Ernest de Sarzec when he reached Basra. Bricks and cones inscribed in an ancient script had been found there, along with the

torso of a statue of a man. Intrigued, Sarzec decided to investigate.

Telloh consisted of a series of mounds stretching along the bank of a dried-up canal surrounded by a wasteland of sunbaked mud. Without even waiting for permission from the Ottoman authorities, Sarzec engaged some local laborers to dig trial trenches into the principal mounds. At some point during this illicit excavation, Sarzec happened to spur his horse up and over the largest mound—about 50 feet high—and noticed a dark stone that appeared to have been shaped by hand. Dismounting to investigate, he found himself examining the shoulder of a large statue.

Under the topsoil of this same mound, Sarzec found a platform of unbaked brick, evidently the foundation of some larger building. In a recess in one of the walls, his workers discovered the torso of the very figure from which the shoulder had come. It was large, too large for Sarzec to remove from the site, so he decided to rebury it for safekeeping until he could mount a proper expedition.

In roughly seven months of excavating in 1877 and 1878, Sarzec made a number of other remarkable discoveries. He uncovered inscribed tablets, jars, and incised cylinder seals—which, when rolled across a surface of damp clay, functioned as signatures, marks of ownership, or badges of office.

The French government subsidized Sarzec's return to Telloh in 1880-1881, during which time he found a whole series of statues carved—like the one he had reburied—from diorite, a hard rock later found to have been quarried far away in Oman and transported up the Persian Gulf. The solemn images were finely sculpted; in their austere and formal beauty, they could stand comparison with the works of almost any period in the history of art. Realizing something of the significance of his finds, Sarzec took leave of absence from his post in 1881 and returned to Paris with his Telloh collection, for which the Louvre museum paid him the then-princely sum of 130,000 French francs.

The museum's money was well spent. Although the Louvre's experts could not fully realize it at the time, the masterpieces they had acquired would provide tangible evidence of a lost civilization—much older than Babylonia or Assyria—whose roots stretched back to the very beginnings of recorded history. For the ancient site that Sarzec had excavated had been a city belonging to a people scholars were beginning to identify tentatively by the name Sumerian. At the time Sarzec brought his haul back to France, the existence of such a

Wearing high boots and a wide-brimmed, white sun hat, Ernest de Sarzec sits on the edge of an excavation at Telloh, flanked by Turkish officials and backed by members of his excavating team, some of them armed against raiding bands from neighboring tribes. The photograph was taken about 1878, when Sarzec was just beginning his long, 20-year exploration of the ancient Sumerian town of Girsu.

culture was still a matter of controversy. Less than a decade had passed since the very name of Sumer had first been rescued from thousands of years of oblivion.

The exhumation of the Sumerian legacy proved a remarkable collective achievement. Starting with a few intrepid adventurers, it was carried forward by the unremitting—and often unrewarded—toil of generations of linguistic scholars, poring over fragmented clay tablets engraved in a puzzling script. While philologists labored in museum basements, archaeologists in the field fleshed out the image of the people who had produced the inscriptions.

Despite the problems of working amid ruins of crumbled mud brick, the archaeologists uncovered a world of temples, palaces, and crowded residential quarters as intricately veined as any Near Eastern bazaar today. The diggers found, too, whole libraries of clay tablets that opened up unexpected mental landscapes. These ancient people had had a literature and a technology of their own; their myths sometimes tantalizingly foreshadowed the Book of Genesis, and their numerical system, based on the number 60, bequeathed the divisions of the hour and the minute in use to this day.

As more became known about them over the course of the ensuing century, the Sumerians finally received their due as one of the great creator civilizations, employing the potter's wheel and plow,

mastering such techniques as riveting, soldering, engraving, and inlaying, and constructing large edifices with the aid of arches, vaults, and domes. Most important of all, the Sumerians inaugurated the era of recorded history by developing its prerequisite, the art of writing. Their cuneiform—literally, wedge-shaped—script was humankind's first medium for expressing language in signs.

The Sumerian homeland seems an unlikely spot for the world's earliest civilization to have flowered. From Baghdad south to the Persian Gulf, the vast, featureless plain would appear to offer little stimulus to the development of a truly urban culture. It is water-laid land, its soil alluvial silt deposited by the seasonal flooding of the Tigris and the Euphrates. Builders here have the benefit of neither stone nor suitable wood for building. Indeed, there is not much vegetation of any kind between the patches of cultivated land, except in spring when the rains have covered the plain in fine grass. For the six summer months, the temperature can reach 125° F. In the words of the great 19th-century English archaeologist Austen Henry Layard, "Desolation meets desolation: a feeling of awe succeeds to wonder; for there is nothing to relieve the mind, to lead to hope, or to tell of what has gone by."

This region—today a sunbaked wilderness of heat, haze, and sudden dust storms—once provided surpluses of foodstuffs, a precondition to the rise of cities. The secret was irrigation. The brown, parched plains contained very fertile soil, enriched by river-borne minerals and organic materials carried down from the headwaters of the Tigris and the Euphrates and spread over the surrounding land by the spring flooding. All that was required to reap a rich harvest was a steady supply of water during the rest of the year.

Irrigation had begun on a small scale in northern Mesopotamia during the sixth millennium. By around 5000 BC, perhaps due to the pressure of a growing population with an increasingly settled lifestyle, an extensive infrastructure of canals, ditches, and basins became necessary. This time, which archaeologists have named the Ubaid period after a small site in southern Mesopotamia, produced spectacular results. Indeed, so fertile was Sumer's flowering that it may well have given rise to the Old Testament tradition of a paradise on earth—the Garden of Eden *(pages 14-17)*.

Apocryphal though that story might be, the fact remains that in Sumer during the fifth millennium BC, people were, for the first time in human history, spared the demands of catching or growing

food for their own sustenance. A farmer could produce more than he or his family needed and could barter the surplus to neighbors who were free to devote themselves to other occupations: to crafts such as pottery and metalworking, to administrative jobs in the world's first bureaucracies, to the service of the gods. So civilization—with all its mixed blessings—was born.

For in their very success lay the seeds of the Sumerians' eventual downfall. The rich cities with their busy markets and stepped temple towers known as ziggurats acted as magnets for rural dwellers, putting a strain on housing and sanitation. Internecine rivalries and warfare among these cities diverted labor and resources from more productive endeavors. Over the centuries the fields on which the residents depended for their nourishment grew less productive, as water—spread across the fields by the irrigation channels—leached salts from the soil and gradually reduced its fertility. Added to the Sumerians' long list of "firsts" must be humankind's earliest example of environmental devastation.

At least partly as a result of this, the political power of Sumer had dissipated by about 2000 BC; the language of its people fell out of general use at around the same time. But the Sumerian culture would not perish completely; rather it would metamorphose and become the basis of the Babylonian civilization, which would inherit both Sumer's legacy and its territory.

Memories of the successor civilizations—Assyria and Persia, as well as Babylonia—were kept alive by the writings of Greek historians such as Herodotus and Xenophon and by references in the Old Testament. So it was that in the 12th century AD a rabbi named Benjamin of Tudela, who traveled from Spain to contact Jewish groups in the Near East, correctly identified ruins he found in the vicinity of the city of Mosul as those of Assyrian Nineveh.

After the European Renaissance of the 15th century had revived interest in classical learning, a Roman named Pietro della Valle explored the mound at Babylon and brought the first examples of cuneiform writing back to Europe. Interest quickened in the 18th century; the probing, inquisitive climate of the Age of Enlightenment stimulated curiosity about the realities of the biblical lands. In time, the European powers, looking for fresh trading opportunities, showed themselves to be eager to improve relations with the Otto-

EDEN: A PARADISE LOST BENEATH THE WATERS?

Just where was Eden? Tradition places the garden in ancient Mesopotamia. Some scholars argue that it lay in southern Iraq; at least one puts it even farther south, lost beneath the waters of the Persian Gulf.

A cuneiform tablet found in the ruins of Nippur suggests a link between Sumerian myth and the biblical story. It speaks of a pure and bright land that knew neither sickness nor death. Into this peaceful realm the water god Enki had fresh water brought so a lush garden might grow. He then begat through the earth-mother goddess Ninhursag three generations of goddesses, all born with painless labor. Ninhursag, in turn, created eight precious plants, which Enki ate. Angry, Ninhursag declared that Enki must die and abandoned him. When eight parts of Enki's body began to fail, a clever fox persuaded Ninhursag to save the water god. Seated beside him, she brought into being a healing deity for each afflicted part, one of which was a rib.

The Sumerian word for rib is *ti,* and the rib-healing goddess came to be called Ninti, which translates both as "the lady of the rib" and "the lady who makes live." This play on words does not work in Hebrew, but the rib

did enter the Garden of Eden story in the form of Eve, the mother of the human race—"the lady who makes live." Interestingly, the words *Eden* and *Adam* also appear in cuneiform. Eden means "uncultivated plain"; Adam, "settlement on the plain."

Beyond the literary and linguistic links between Eden and Sumer is the evidence of geography. As told in Genesis, "A river went out of Eden to water the garden; and from thence it was parted, and became into four heads." One was the Euphrates; a second, the Tigris. But the locations of the other two, the Gihon and the Pison, have long confounded scholars. Juris Zarins of Southwest Missouri State University believes that a river now

In both Sumerian and Hebrew creation myths, man is wrought from clay. This cuneiform tablet from Nippur relates how the water god Enki ordered his mother, Nammu, to form man from "the clay that is over the abyss."

Humankind's all too brief sojourn in Eden is depicted in Lucas Cranach the Elder's narrative painting of 1530. The German Renaissance master, known for his religious themes and vibrant colors, chose to portray each step in the well-known drama simultaneously. In the foreground, God gives Adam and Eve dominion over the Garden. At far right, He molds Adam from clay; and at near right, Satan, half-man, half-serpent, tempts the couple with the forbidden fruit. At top center, God forms Eve from Adam's rib. To the left of this scene, Adam and Eve, having sinned by eating of the Tree of Knowledge, hide their nakedness from the Lord. Finally, an angel brandishing a sword drives the pair from Eden.

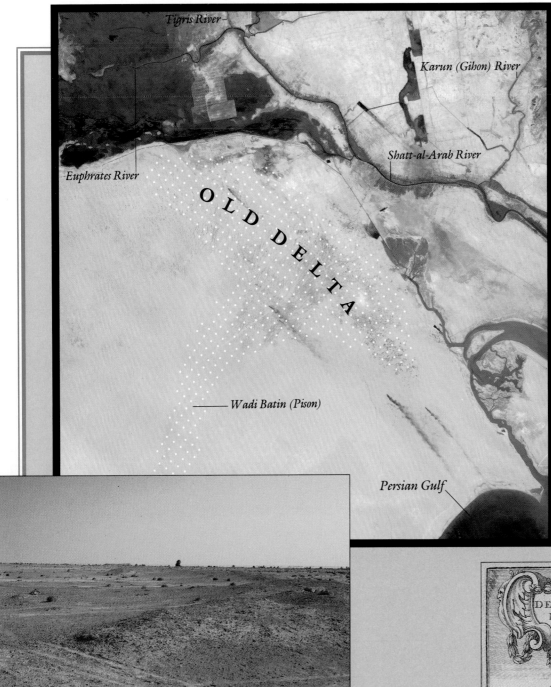

Tigris River

Karun (Gihon) River

Euphrates River

Shatt-al-Arab River

OLD DELTA

Wadi Batin (Pison)

Persian Gulf

A satellite photograph of Saudi Arabia confirms the existence of all four rivers Zarins identifies with the Genesis story. At upper left the Tigris and the Euphrates merge to form the Shatt-al-Arab, the channel into which the modern Karun, or biblical Gihon, flows. In the Saudi Arabian desert lie the remains of a delta and a river system called the Wadi Batin and Wadi Rimah, which Zarins assumes is the ancient Pison.

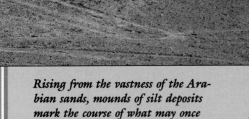

Rising from the vastness of the Arabian sands, mounds of silt deposits mark the course of what may once have been the Pison River.

A 1691 French map of Mesopotamia, showing Eden at lower right, records the region's waterways fairly accurately. But the mapmaker, trying to include all of Eden's rivers, wrongly named the arteries of the Persian Gulf delta as the Pison and Gehan.

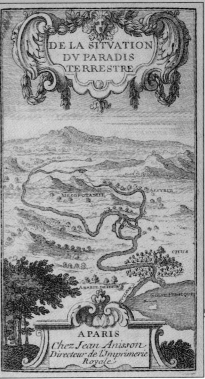

named Karun, rising in Iran and flowing toward the Persian Gulf, is the Gihon and that a dry riverbed in the Saudi Arabian desert once held the Pison. According to Zarins, Eden was located at the confluence of the four rivers in the Persian Gulf region. This, he points out, was an area that 32,000 years ago enjoyed a salubrious climate but by 15,000 BC had become arid, forcing the foragers who lived there to migrate. Around 6000-5000 BC the climate changed again, and the arid reaches of eastern and northeastern Saudi Arabia and southwestern Iran blossomed anew. Zarins proposes that foragers returned to the area and encountered early farmers—Ubaid ancestors of the Sumerians. As these nomads stopped their roaming and settled down to an agricultural life, in what must have been a period of severe adjustment for them, Zarins theorizes, they may well have passed on a traditional tale of a paradise lost millennia ago—a place where people had been able to live off the land without having to till the soil.

But how did this Eden wind up at the bottom of the Persian Gulf? Juris Zarins thinks that rising sea levels, brought about by the gradual melting of glaciers in the wake of the last great ice age, submerged it some 7,000 years ago.

man Empire, which had controlled Mesopotamia since the 1530s.

Travelers to the region found a culture in decline. The land between the rivers was by now a remote and neglected province of a power that had seen better days. The ruling sultan was a thousand miles away in Constantinople; locally, authority devolved on officials who were more interested in extorting taxes to line their own pockets than in promoting the rule of law. One is said to have succinctly instructed his revenue collectors to "Go! Destroy! Eat!"

As a result, bandits joined disease and discomfort among the hazards awaiting the early voyagers. Nevertheless, a few courageous individuals braved the dangers. The Abbé Beauchamp, the pope's vicar-general to the region, made the first excavations at Babylon in the 1780s. His memoirs, including descriptions of the inscribed bricks he found there, attracted widespread interest back in Europe.

Even more significantly, the king of Denmark commissioned an expedition to the Near East in 1756 "for the advancement of knowledge." Five of its six members died there of disease, but the sixth, a German named Carsten Niebuhr, reached the 2,000-year-old ruined palace of the kings of Persia at Persepolis in present-day Iran and took careful copies of the inscriptions there. Published in 1772, the information he brought back proved a crucial first step in the long chain of scholarship that led to the rediscovery of Sumer.

The Persepolis inscriptions were—as Niebuhr was the first to realize—written in three different languages, all of which employed the same cuneiform script. The inscriptions were too brief to allow for adequate decipherment of two of the languages, but the third eventually yielded its secrets. It turned out to be Old Persian, the language of Iran between the sixth and fourth centuries BC. Many individuals contributed to its mastering, but none more so than a German high-school teacher, Georg Friedrich Grotefend, whose interest was aroused in 1802 as the result of a bet with a friend.

Through his knowledge of Greek historical texts, Grotefend was familiar with a formula, used by the later Persian kings in monumental inscriptions, that ran: "X, Great King, King of Kings, Son of Y, Great King." With that in mind, he examined the Persepolis inscriptions for repetitions of symbols that paralleled this form of address. He not only found what he was looking for but also came upon a clue that helped him identify the individual monarchs named. For the wording he discovered apparently read: "X, Great King, King of Kings, Son of Y, Great King, King of Kings, Son of Z."

To Grotefend the conclusion was obvious. Z, whoever he may have been, had not been a king himself, otherwise the usual formula would have been repeated for him, too. Grotefend needed to trace two Persian kings who had been, respectively, the grandson and the son of a commoner. Armed with this hypothesis, he searched for suitable candidates in Herodotus's king list of the Achaemenid dynasty, which ruled during the Old Persian period. He soon found them: Hystaspes, a nonroyal provincial governor under Cyrus the Great, had fathered a king, the great Darius, who had in turn sired another ruler, Xerxes. In a matter of months, Grotefend had not merely identified the Persian words for "king," "son," and "great" but had also determined the cuneiform names of three crucial figures in Persian history.

While Grotefend and others were working on the decipherment of Old Persian, political conditions were changing in Mesopotamia itself. Relations between the European powers and the Ottomans evolved to the point where the British decided in 1798 that they needed permanent diplomatic representation in Baghdad; and, in 1802, the British resident in Baghdad received consular accreditation. A succession of distinguished linguists and scholars held the position of British resident in the city, and the residency in which they lived rapidly became a headquarters for archaeological enterprise in Mesopotamia.

In intellectual stature and scholarly achievement, the greatest of the 19th-century residents was a soldier, diplomat, and linguist named Henry Creswicke Rawlinson. Rawlinson originally traveled east in 1826 as a soldier in Britain's Indian army. He challenged all comers for a substantial stake at "running, jumping, quoits, racquets, billiards, pigeon-shooting, pig-sticking, steeple-chasing, chess, and games of skill at cards." Later in his career, he rode 750 miles across the Persian desert in six days on a diplomatic mission.

Rawlinson was a notable example of that rarest of types, the man of action who by intellectual application turns himself into a scholar. Fittingly, his part in the rediscovery of Sumer combined scholarship and adventure in equal measure. For if Grotefend and his cohorts had begun to crack the mysteries of Old Persian, they had been stymied by the other languages of the Persepolis inscriptions.

Posted to Persia on military duty in 1835, Rawlinson heard of rock carvings near the little town of Behistun. There he found not merely heroic relief sculptures celebrating the deeds of King Darius

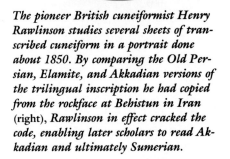

The pioneer British cuneiformist Henry Rawlinson studies several sheets of transcribed cuneiform in a portrait done about 1850. By comparing the Old Persian, Elamite, and Akkadian versions of the trilingual inscription he had copied from the rockface at Behistun in Iran (right), Rawlinson in effect cracked the code, enabling later scholars to read Akkadian and ultimately Sumerian.

but, more importantly, about 1,200 lines of cuneiform text describing his achievements in—once again, as at Persepolis—three different languages. Rawlinson realized the inscriptions might provide a key to the two so-far undeciphered languages, but he was faced by severe practical problems in copying them.

The carvings were more than 300 feet up a cliff face, and it proved impracticable to transcribe them from ground level, even with the aid of a telescope. Rawlinson made a series of visits over the years to transcribe the inscriptions. He would carry a ladder up the cliff, managing to perch it on a ledge about two feet wide at the base of the inscriptions. To record the upper lines of the first section—

A modern photograph shows the huge bas-reliefs carved around 520 BC on the cliff face at Behistun, along with the panels of cuneiform writing Rawlinson repeatedly risked his life to copy. Situated 340 feet above the ground for all to see, the reliefs depict the triumphant Persian king Darius, third from left, standing in judgment over 10 rebel chiefs. The inscriptions list his achievements.

which turned out to be Old Persian—Rawlinson had to stand on the top rung and support himself against the rockface with one elbow while he committed the symbols to his notebook. "The interest of the occupation entirely did away with any sense of danger," he later wrote modestly.

The other two inscription blocks posed even greater problems. The ledge had broken away under one section, and Rawlinson had to use his ladder to bridge the gap. There was a heart-stopping moment as he crawled across the rungs; one side of the ladder gave way, leaving him hanging by his fingers over the chasm. He reached the far side hand over hand and set up a more stable scaffold to complete his task.

The last inscription, the most inaccessible of all, at first defeated even his ingenuity, until in 1847, "a wild Kurdish boy" volunteered for a fee to scramble across the almost sheer face of the inscription carrying a rope. This was duly attached to pegs at each side, and a sort of bosun's chair was suspended from the rope. The boy was then hauled inch by inch across the face of the carving, taking papier-mâché imprints of the carvings under Rawlinson's direction.

The Behistun inscriptions opened the way to the translation of one of the two unknown languages. Rawlinson had undertaken the task himself when he became the British resident to Baghdad in December 1843. He built a summerhouse overhanging the river Tigris at the bottom of the residency garden. To counter the oppressive heat, he rigged up a waterwheel that doused the wooden building continually with river water. There he would sit with a pet lion cub drowsing under his chair, working on the decipherment of the cuneiform texts even in the hottest months of summer.

Rawlinson eventually identified the language in the casts made by the daring Kurdish boy as Babylonian, a later dialect of Akkadian, the language first written down by a Semitic people who had established themselves in Mesopotamia alongside the Sumerians by the third millennium BC. Indeed, the landmark publication in Akkadian decipherment was Rawlinson's provisional translation of the Babylonian text from Behistun in 1851.

Rawlinson was in the right place at the right time, for Mesopotamian archaeology was about to become headline news across Europe thanks to the excavation of three enormous mounds in the north of the country. While serving as the French consular agent in the

French diplomat Paul Emile Botta, discoverer in 1843 of the forgotten Assyrian capital at Khorsabad built by Sargon II, knew the Near East quite well, having explored much of Arabia and Yemen before turning his attention to archaeology. His digs at Khorsabad were often frustrated by corrupt Turkish officials; the city was not systematically excavated until the 20th century.

Unearthed by Botta at Khorsabad, the 15-foot-tall alabaster carving at right portrays a bearded figure holding a lion cub and a knife. Botta shipped this and other heavy sculptures to Paris's Louvre by floating them down the Tigris on rafts, then loading them on vessels that—since the Suez Canal had yet to be dug—made the long voyage to France around the Cape of Good Hope.

northern Iraqi city of Mosul in 1843, Paul Emile Botta found the remains of an ancient palace nearby. That site, Khorsabad, turned out to be Dur Sharrukin, the capital of Assyrian king Sargon II at the end of the eighth century BC. From it, Botta salvaged huge sculptures of human-headed winged bulls and lions and a seemingly endless sequence of finely carved bas-reliefs of gods, kings, and battles.

A couple of years later, Austen Henry Layard exposed the remains of eight palaces of the Assyrian kings at Nimrud. He returned in 1849 to explore a mound called Kuyunjik, which turned out to be the greatest of the Assyrian capitals, the city of Nineveh. Over the next few months he found, in his words, "no less than seventy-one halls, chambers and passages, whose walls, almost without exception, had been panelled with slabs of sculptured alabaster recording the wars, the triumphs, and the great deeds of the Assyrian king. By a rough calculation, about 9,880 feet, or nearly two miles, of bas-reliefs, with 27 portals, formed by colossal winged bulls and lion-sphinxes, were uncovered in that part alone of the building explored during my researches." One of his most significant discoveries was the library assembled by the seventh-century BC monarch Ashurbanipal, the most learned of Assyria's kings. In all, some 24,000 tablets bearing cuneiform inscriptions were recovered.

The discoveries caused a sensation in the archaeologists' home countries. Botta's finds, laboriously transported back to France at the cost of considerable loss and breakage en route, went on display in 1847 in a special Assyrian Museum at the Louvre, and the British Museum showed the results of Layard's work the following year.

The excavations at Khorsabad, Nimrud, and Nineveh radically altered humankind's views of its own past. The new science of Assyriology was born to interpret the significance of the finds. Meanwhile, in Mesopotamia, a rush for antiquities began. Treasure seekers representing great foreign museums traveled from mound to mound, tunneling feverishly in the hope of finding fresh booty.

Archaeological exploration was not a job for the

fainthearted in 19th-century Mesopotamia. Conditions were particularly difficult in the old Sumerian heartland to the south. The landscape was so bandit infested that Ottoman rulers made visitors sign a letter absolving the authorities of any responsibility for safety. Wild animals, too, were a problem; when the English archaeologist William Kennett Loftus set up camp in 1849, he was troubled nightly by a family of lions, who killed off the team's guard dogs one by one, the last only a few feet from his tent.

In the mid-1850s this frenetic burst of activity was interrupted by the Crimean War. By the time the war was over, interest in archaeological exploration in the area had waned. Instead the focus of attention turned back to the decipherment of the various cuneiform languages. With the tablets recovered from Ashurbanipal's library, the linguistic detectives now had a surfeit of material.

Like the buildings that housed them, the tablets were made of clay. The cuneiform symbols were impressed in the still-damp mud with a reed stylus, and the tablet was left to dry in the sun. The results proved unexpectedly durable, although breakage caused some problems for the scholars who sought to translate the tablets so long after they had been written.

By this stage scholars studying the cuneiform scripts had a working knowledge of Old Persian and had made substantial progress with the decipherment of Akkadian. Given the existence of the trilingual inscriptions from Persepolis and Behistun, the problem of cracking the third language might have been expected to be an easy one. In fact it was anything but. This third language, Elamite, would not be deciphered until some decades later. The Elamites, with their principal city at Susa, inhabited southwestern Iran from earliest times and were the predecessors of the Persians in that region. Elamite turned out to have no similarity to any other known tongue; even now it is only partially understood.

The Akkadian inscriptions attracted particular attention in the light of the Nineveh discoveries, because Akkadian was the language of the Assyrians as it had been of the Babylonians. Rawlinson and others soon learned that the script consisted of several hundred different symbols; some of them were apparently logograms—a sort of shorthand sign denoting an entire word, much as *&* is used in English to represent the word *and*—others were phonetic, representing sounds. Therefore, attempts to work out a simple Akkadian alphabet proved to be fruitless.

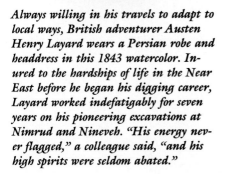

Always willing in his travels to adapt to local ways, British adventurer Austen Henry Layard wears a Persian robe and headdress in this 1843 watercolor. Inured to the hardships of life in the Near East before he began his digging career, Layard worked indefatigably for seven years on his pioneering excavations at Nimrud and Nineveh. "His energy never flagged," a colleague said, "and his high spirits were seldom abated."

One of Rawlinson's contemporaries, a reclusive Irish theologian named Edward Hincks, realized that the symbols did not represent individual letters but rather syllables combining vowel and consonant sounds. For example, seven different signs that earlier scholars had identified with the letter *r* in fact represented *ar, ir, er, ur, ra, ri,* and *ru.* Hincks also established that the same symbol could have more than one meaning. Some signs could, in different contexts, serve either as logograms or phonetic symbols. More confusingly still, Rawlinson, working independently, discovered that certain signs could represent more than one syllable and conversely that some syllables could be transcribed by several different signs. One extreme case—the syllable *du*—could be written in no fewer than 23 different ways.

Translating the language was a puzzle fit to try the finest intellects. In 1857 William Henry Fox Talbot, a well-known pioneer of photography and an eager Assyriologist, wrote to the Royal Asiatic Society to suggest a test of the reliability of the scholars' efforts to date. He was working on an unpublished Assyrian text, and at his

Massive winged lions with bearded human heads and the horned crowns of divinity guard a monumental entrance at Nimrud in a watercolor done in 1850 by Frederick Cooper, an artist assigned to Layard's second expedition to Mesopotamia. In all, Layard unearthed 13 pairs of such colossal statues, managing to ship two of the 10-ton figures to the British Museum in London.

suggestion, copies were sent to Rawlinson, Hincks, and the leading French Assyriologist, Jules Oppert. Each was asked to translate it without consulting the others. Skeptics expected that the results would reveal broad discrepancies. In fact, when the society's committee examined the submissions six weeks later, it found them to tally in all essential details. The mysteries of Akkadian were finally being penetrated.

Yet increased understanding of the language in some respects only heightened the scholars' bafflement. The more they learned about written Akkadian, the odder, in some respects, it seemed to be. When Egyptian hieroglyphs had been deciphered earlier in the century, a direct relationship had quickly been established between the symbols and the pictographic word signs that had been their origins. With Akkadian that proved not to be the case.

In addition, linguists quickly noted similarities between Akkadian and such later Semitic tongues as Hebrew and Arabic. Still, cuneiform seemed poorly adapted to the patterns of Semitic speech, making no allowance, for example, for the variable vowel sounds that are a feature of all the Semitic languages. There were odd omissions, too. Akkadian had no specific symbol for lion, even though lions were common in Assyrian territory; instead a symbol meaning "large dog" had been adopted to fill the bill. These quirks had led Hincks to suggest as early as 1850 that the Akkadian-speaking Semitic inhabitants of Assyria and Babylonia did not invent cuneiform. Instead, he surmised, they might have borrowed the script from some earlier non-Semitic people and adapted it as best they could to represent their own speech patterns.

Support for Hincks's hypothesis would come from some interesting texts that Layard had unearthed among the contents of Ashurbanipal's library. These so-called syllabaries listed now familiar Akkadian terms alongside unknown words, also written in cuneiform script, in yet another unidentified language. In an 1855 lecture, Rawlinson surmised that the speakers of the unknown tongue might have been cuneiform's originators.

Still, the mystery of the people behind the script remained. Rawlinson mistakenly labeled them Babylonian Scyths, nomads who once inhabited the lands north of the Black Sea. It was left to Jules Oppert to name them correctly. In an 1869 lecture he suggested that they were Sumerians, basing his conclusion on the title "king of Sumer and Akkad" that appears in some Akkadian inscriptions.

Lady Layard, wife of the great archaeologist, wears a necklace and earrings made of engraved cylinder seals—used in ancient Mesopotamia for identification purposes—that her husband-to-be brought back from the Near East and presented to her as a wedding gift. As more and more Assyrian relics reached Europe, they influenced fashion and inspired a decorative style known as Assyrian revival.

Freestanding figures and bas-reliefs line one of the galleries in the Louvre displaying the treasures of Sumerian and Assyrian sculpture shipped to Paris by a succession of 19th-century French archaeologists, including Paul Emile Botta and Ernest de Sarzec. The excitement and curiosity such pieces elicited among the public helped prompt the large and more systematic archaeological expeditions launched in the 20th century.

Oppert's inspired guess did not at once win universal approval. A number of scholars, led by the Frenchman Joseph Halévy, insisted that the Sumerians did not exist. In the opposition's view, the language of the syllabaries found at Nineveh was no more than an archaic form of Akkadian used for religious and other ceremonial purposes. While linguists argued the point in academic journals, a fresh breakthrough in decipherment diverted public attention from Sumer back to more northerly parts of Mesopotamia.

Throughout the 1850s and 1860s the slow process of sorting and translating the clay tablets from Nineveh had proceeded at the British Museum. One of the institution's most accomplished readers of cuneiform was a shy young man named George Smith, who had been an engraver's apprentice before his passion for Assyriology won him a position in the museum's Department of Oriental Antiquities. He was working through a pile of fragmented tablets that he had provisionally labeled "Mythology," when his eyes fell on something that greatly excited him. So unbridled was his enthusiasm that, as his astonished colleagues in the department's study room looked on, he distractedly started removing his clothes. What he had found, in a

section of a broken tablet, was nothing less than an Akkadian version of the biblical story of the Flood.

Smith revealed his discovery in a lecture to the Biblical Archaeological Society in December 1872 before an audience that included Britain's prime minister, William Gladstone. The tablet described how a king named Utnapishtim survived a great flood sent to punish humankind by building a ship into which he loaded his family and animals. After six days and nights of rain, the weather cleared and his boat ran aground on a mountainside. Utnapishtim, like Noah, then sent out a bird—in the Assyrian version a raven, not a dove—which did not return, indicating that it had found dry land.

The obvious similarities with the Book of Genesis aroused widespread public interest. Sensing a scoop, a British newspaper, the *Daily Telegraph,* offered the museum a substantial sum of money to dispatch Smith to Nineveh in quest of the rest of the tablet. He spent more than three months traveling and visiting other sites before setting to work in the area where Layard had found the library. By one of archaeology's great coincidences, Smith unearthed the missing lines within a week.

George Smith was perhaps more fortunate than he would have wished, for the *Telegraph* promptly proclaimed his mission accomplished and closed down the dig. The museum managed to raise the funds to send him back for a second, highly productive excavating season. On a third trip, however, he contracted dysentery

SUMERIAN FASHIONS REBORN

Although their garments perished with their mortal remains thousands of years ago, the Sumerians nevertheless left a record in their art of the clothing they wore. During the earlier phase of the culture's development, both men and women dressed in wool or linen knee- to calf-length skirts known as *kaunakes,* some of which were tiered or fringed. Archaeologists digging at Susa discovered remnants of linen clinging to copper axes dating from the fourth millennium BC that revealed such an accomplished degree of weaving skill that the pieces compared

while trying to cross the Syrian desert in the heat of summer and died.

In the wake of Smith's dramatic Assyrian discoveries, the controversy over the existence of Sumer might have attracted little notice had it not been for Sarzec's excavations at Telloh and the concrete evidence they provided of Sumerian civilization in its heyday. Buoyed by his first season of digging, Sarzec returned to Telloh the following year, as he would each year thereafter almost until the end of the century. His later discoveries included nine more large diorite statues—subsequently revealed to be 4,000 years old—along with numerous bas-reliefs and inscriptions. Best of all, he dug up the celebrated Stele of the Vultures—a bas-relief of a king leading his army—that predated the other Telloh finds by several hundred years and constituted the earliest representation of military force ever discovered up to that time.

The Frenchman was by no means the first European to have dug in the Sumerian heartland. Besides the lion-plagued Loftus, another Englishman, J. E. Taylor—who like Sarzec was a consular official in Basra—had in 1854 tunneled into the remains of a ziggurat near the Euphrates that the Roman traveler della Valle had visited in 1625. Taylor discovered inscribed cylinder seals buried in the foundations that permitted Rawlinson to identify the site as Ur of the Chaldees, which the Bible lists as the hometown of the patriarch Abraham.

favorably to modern linen.

As time wore on, a long, shawl-like garment appeared. Perhaps designed for ceremonial use, it was worn by draping a length of cloth over the left shoulder, wrapping it around the back, under the right arm, over the left shoulder, and then again under the right armpit. In the two photographs taken in the 1930s *(right and left)*, French models at L'Ecole des Beaux-Arts display re-created male and female versions of the shawl. For the woman's costume, the seamstress used a 14-foot-long, 4-foot-wide piece of cloth. The man's pose was based on the statue of Gudea on page 155, with hands folded in the gesture of respect still seen in Asia today.

By Sarzec's day, there were many people in Mesopotamia who recognized the financial, if not the historical, value of the discoveries. A flourishing black market in antiquities developed, and the Baghdad dealers viewed Telloh as a rich supply source. Each year when Sarzec wound up his operations, freelancers swarmed in to tunnel for treasure. In this way an entire library of Sumerian texts, comparable in size to the collection Layard had discovered at Nineveh, was located and concealed from the Frenchman. Some 35,000 tablets found their way onto the Baghdad market and, from there, to private collectors and museums in Europe and America.

The evidence that emerged from Telloh by both licit and illicit channels convinced most scholars that Oppert had been right in directing attention to the Sumerians. Of Sarzec's work, Oppert himself declared in a speech to the Fifth International Congress of Orientalists in 1881 that "since the discovery of Nineveh no discovery has been made which compares in importance with the recent excavations." Suddenly the hunt was on to learn more of what was now recognized as humankind's first urban civilization.

A protégé of Henry Rawlinson's, George Smith—seen above wearing a beard of almost Assyrian luxuriance—had such a facility for Akkadian that he could read ancient inscriptions almost as fast as someone perusing a modern newspaper.

Prior to 1880 Mesopotamian archaeology had been almost exclusively the preserve of the British and the French. Then new players arrived on the scene. In 1886 a team led by the German archaeologist Robert Koldeway excavated two sites—Surghul and El Hibba—only 12 miles from Telloh, beginning the pioneering work Koldeway would continue in the ruins of Babylon from 1899 to 1913. The Germans' scientific approach to these digs constituted a revolution in technique, which the eminent British archaeologist Seton Lloyd called a "new phase in the history of archaeology."

Excavators began to recognize the importance of a mound's stratigraphy—the sequence of its layers—in unraveling the complexities of its history. Increasingly, they dug stratigraphic pits that provided a chronological cross section of life on the site throughout its history. By recording the objects according to the layer of occupation in which they were found—particularly pottery sherds, which were abundant, durable, and liable to frequent changes in style and technique—researchers could cross date the various levels of habitation with those of other sites elsewhere.

In 1889 the first American expedition arrived in Mesopotamia and started work at Nippur, a massive mound in a desolate region

midway between Baghdad and the Persian Gulf. The effort was the brainchild of the Reverend John P. Peters, recently appointed professor of Hebrew at the University of Pennsylvania.

Despite more than the usual share of hardships and disasters, the team remained on the site for a dozen years, although for a while it appeared the Americans might not survive the first season's digging. There was trouble in Constantinople getting permits, followed by problems with the official appointed to supervise the excavation, who turned out to be deeply involved in the black market. But the most serious difficulties were with the tribesmen living nearby.

Relations were bad from the beginning; the Americans narrowly evaded a raiding party as the expedition first approached Nippur. Installed on the site, they found that privacy was hard to come by as their Arab neighbors wandered through the camp at will. Locally hired diggers traded insults with the Turkish guards who were assigned to the excavation. Food was stolen and a bread oven destroyed. Things came to a head when tribesmen raided the camp at night in an attempt to steal the expedition's horses. One of the raiders was shot dead by a guard. Realizing that retaliation was inevitable, the archaeologists closed down work for the season and prepared to withdraw. But before they could leave, the dead man's relatives staged a nocturnal raid and set fire to the camp's reed huts. In the ensuing confusion, half the horses died, and the team's weapons and a thousand dollars in gold were plundered. The archaeologists counted themselves lucky to escape with their lives.

Peters refused to give up. Returning the next year, he found that drought and an epidemic of cholera had changed the mood of the local tribesmen, who saw their misfortunes as retribution magically

Cracked and pieced together, this tablet is one of 12 from Nineveh that recounts the wondrous adventures of Gilgamesh, a semidivine king of the Sumerian city of Uruk. Blessed by luck, George Smith, who studied the tablets, found not only the lines that filled in the missing portion detailing a flood similar to the Great Flood of the Bible but also, at a later date, a fragment that contained, as he put it, "the story of man's original innocence, of the temptation, and of the fall."

inflicted by the Americans. They now seemed delighted to welcome the foreigners back; no mention was made of the events of the previous year, and the digging commenced. The site soon began to yield inscribed tablets in large numbers. Unfortunately for later generations of archaeologists, Peters did not heed the new scientific approach to excavation that the Germans had introduced. He kept scanty records and made no detailed drawings. He just sent his work crews scurrying about helter-skelter to whichever site looked the most promising for tablets.

The American campaign continued—under new leadership as of 1893—but conditions in the field remained difficult. The temperature still rose to 120° F in summer, and sandstorms were frequent. During a subsequent digging season, a young member of the team died of dysentery and malaria. To cap it all, there was political unrest. The local tribes rebelled against the Turkish authorities and fighting broke out in the immediate vicinity. On occasion the Arab diggers would drop their baskets, seize their weapons, and head off into battle shouting war cries.

Despite all the troubles, the excavations continued until 1900.

Surrounded by a camel-thorn fence to keep out hostile locals, the camp set up by the first American expedition to Mesopotamia swelters at the Sumerian city of Nippur in an 1890 photograph. Over the course of a decade, the University of Pennsylvania team managed to unearth some 30,000 clay tablets at Nippur, but as a picture that was taken the same year attests (right), their methods left much to be desired. Here, the archaeologists have dug through ruins spanning two millennia with little regard for the telling sequence of occupation levels.

The Americans' utter unpreparedness, naiveté, and lack of a realistic appreciation of conditions in that harsh land often led to chaos and turmoil, but the result of their pertinacity was the recovery of an extraordinary wealth of knowledge as well as artifacts. They uncovered about 30,000 tablets, among them important literary texts, scientific works, king lists, even multiplication tables for every number from 1 to 1,350. There were collections of proverbs, some with a sardonic ring to them that still strikes a chord today: "You can have a lord, you can have a king, but the man to fear is the tax collector!" "Friendship lasts a day, kinship endures forever." "For his pleasure: marriage. On his thinking it over: divorce."

With a similar mass of data emerging yearly from Telloh, the evidence for an understanding of Sumerian civilization was now available to scholars. Although Halévy continued to publish articles denying the existence of the Sumerians, by the turn of the century his was a lonely voice; the discoveries at Telloh and Nippur were too persuasive. It became apparent not only that the Sumerians had existed but that they had attained a high level of material and intellectual culture. Scholarship and exploration had combined to push the horizons of history much further back.

The First World War interrupted fieldwork in Mesopotamia. After the end of hostilities, archaeologists returned to find a very different political atmosphere. The Ottoman Empire had crumbled, and Arab nationalism had suddenly become a force to be reckoned with. The League of Nations gave the British—who had captured Baghdad from the Turks in 1917 and occupied most of Iraq as far north as Mosul by November 1918—a temporary mandate to administer Iraq until it could be brought to

full independence. (In 1932 Iraq was admitted to the league as the first fully independent Arab state.)

During British rule, control over archaeological affairs in Mesopotamia rested in the hands of an energetic and scholarly woman named Gertrude Bell. She supervised the drafting of a new law that condoned only properly constituted foreign expeditions, equipped with such experts as architects, photographers, and epigraphists—specialists in copying and translating inscriptions. Bell granted permits for single sites whose exact limits were clearly defined. At the same time, she set up an Iraqi Antiquities Service to establish a collection for a national museum. Archaeological finds henceforth would be shared between the excavators who discovered them and the fledgling state. The days of random treasure hunting were over.

The authorities welcomed foreign expeditions willing to adhere to the new guidelines, resulting in an upsurge of archaeological activity. By the 1920s the archaeologists' own aims and methods had changed profoundly. Although statues, bas-reliefs, and clay tablets continued to turn up in large numbers, the emphasis was no longer on the discovery of objects for their own sake. Increasingly, scientists sought solutions to the great problems raised by the rediscovery of Sumer, problems that touched on such fundamental questions as how and where agriculture was born, why people first grouped together in cities, and what led to the birth of writing.

Stratigraphic digging had been pioneered before the First World War by the Germans under Koldeway excavating at Babylon and at the Assyrian city of Assur. The usefulness of this approach was dramatically demonstrated at the site Rawlinson had identified as Ur by an expedition jointly sponsored by the British Museum and the University of Pennsylvania and under the direction of the British archaeologist Sir Leonard Woolley.

In 1929 Woolley decided to dig a trial pit—starting from the bottom of his earlier excavation of the royal cemetery—down to the lowest levels of the Ur mound in order to learn something of the city's origins. After cutting through three feet of occupational debris, his diggers hit sterile river mud *(pages 88-89)*. Woolley calculated that the mud was above the original level of the surrounding plain. One possible explanation could have been that he had reached the top of a natural hillock "hidden" by the larger, man-made mound of the city that had been built atop it.

But Woolley commanded his crew to keep on digging. Re-

luctantly, they complied. Sure enough, the record of human habitation recommenced eight feet further down. Sensing an important discovery, Woolley summoned two of his assistants to the pit. They could suggest no explanation for the abrupt break in the archaeological record. Then he asked his wife. She announced casually, "Well, of course, it's the Flood."

Further excavations across the site led Woolley initially to concur. In late Ubaid times, he surmised, an immense, silt-bearing flood had covered much of the land of Sumer, destroying hundreds of towns. This, then, he thought, had to be the disaster that had given rise to Sumerian accounts of the Deluge. These had, in turn, been handed down to the Assyrian scribes who had copied the Babylonian chronicle of the Flood and so, eventually, to the story of Noah. "It was not a universal deluge," Woolley wrote, "it was a vast flood in the valley of the Tigris and Euphrates which drowned the whole of the habitable land between the mountains and the desert; for the people who lived there, that was all the world."

Since Woolley's day, scholars have dismissed his identification of the flood layer at Ur with the Deluge of Sumerian legend. *The Epic of Gilgamesh,* the great Babylonian literary work that incorporates an earlier Sumerian version of the flood story, associates the Deluge with the Sumerian king Utnapishtim who reigned at Shurrupak, 70 miles north of Ur, in the early third millennium, much later than the date Woolley had given for his flood. (This is the version that had incited George Smith to disrobe in the British Museum's reading room.) Excavations at Shurrupak have indeed revealed evidence of a flood at about that time. The present consensus is that what Woolley discovered was not proof of *the* Flood so much as evidence of one particularly disastrous inundation in an area where flooding was endemic and where similar catastrophes could have entered the nation's collective memory in the form of legend.

While Woolley was excavating Ur, other sites in Mesopotamia were being examined with similar dili-

British scholar and adventurer Gertrude Bell, who insisted archaeology in Iraq be put on a more professional footing, stands outside her tent at Babylon in 1909. Daughter of a wealthy and powerful family of English industrialists, she became a political officer in the employ of the Crown and used her influence as well as her knowledge of Arabic and Arab ways to help her government establish the kingdom of Iraq after World War I.

gence by other well-equipped teams of specialists. If the 19th century had been the heroic age of Mesopotamian archaeology, conducted largely on the initiative of enterprising individuals following hunches, the 1920s and 1930s were the golden age of the professional archaeologist, working with backing from academic institutions.

The University of Chicago financed digs at several sites along the Diyala River east of Baghdad, discovering Sumerian statues in this provincial region in numbers not seen since the early days at Telloh. A German team explored Uruk, where it found the stunning remains of a Sumerian city dating back to the fourth millennium BC. British and American archaeologists discovered a Sumerian palace and cemetery at Kish, and the French reopened work at Sarzec's old stomping ground of Telloh.

The situation changed again after Iraq attained independence. A new antiquities law passed in 1934 made it difficult for excavators to take artifacts out of the country. As a result, several expeditions moved their operations over the border into Syria, where less stringent rules applied. Nevertheless, important Sumerian discoveries continued to be made in Iraq both by foreign teams and, increasingly, by Iraqis under the aegis of the Iraq Antiquities Directorate.

In any case, enough had already come to light from the mounds of southern Mesopotamia to suggest the scope of the Sumerian achievement in all its grandeur and complexity. Archaeologists had uncovered a whole, intricate world that no one could have dreamed of a century before. True, they had found few great buildings to rival the Parthenon or the pyramids, for unbaked mud brick could not stand the wear of the centuries as well as stone. Yet scientific investigation established that Sumer was deserving of the right to be called the first urban, literate civilization in the history of the world. And there were the voices of the Sumerians themselves, speaking from the tablets, to prove it *(pages 132-133)*.

Finally, as though the reconstitution of Sumer itself was not achievement enough, the archaeologists had dug deeper to find traces of Sumer's own antecedents, shadowy preliterate cultures known only by the names of the sites from which came the fragmentary remains of their houses and their pottery. Sumer had a prehistory of its own. The civilization that had briefly seemed a fixed point on history's far horizon now opened up fresh vistas receding back into unrecorded time. The quest, it seemed, had not ended. The mounds still had other secrets to reveal.

CITIES IN THE SAND

Standing atop the 4,000-year-old ruins of the great ziggurat at Ur, the archaeologist Sir Leonard Woolley was stirred by the melancholy sight before him. To the north and west and south as far as he could see stretched a wasteland of sand. "It seems incredible," Woolley wrote, "that such a wilderness should ever have been habitable for man, and yet the weathered hillocks at one's feet cover the temples and houses of a very great city." And beyond Ur—where now there is only desolation—green, fresh fields checkered the countryside.

Around 5000 BC ancient peoples began to make use of the waters of the Euphrates River to irrigate the fertile but otherwise arid soil of the plain. They also grazed sheep and goats on the desert scrub that surrounded the well-watered fields and gleaned a rich harvest of fish and wildlife from the marshes at the head of the Persian Gulf. So successful were the early inhabitants of the region that over the next three millennia powerful city-states such as Uruk, Ur, and Nippur *(above)* arose in Mesopotamia. Constructed of mud brick, these early cities each housed tens of thousands of inhabitants.

Ironically, the very techniques that had allowed people to flourish in the area also contributed to the cities' eventual decline. Intensive irrigation caused salinization of the soil, with marked decreases in crop production. Constant internecine squabbles between the great city-states over control of the land and water left them too weak to resist one another's depredations and the onslaughts of foreign intruders. Even the life-giving river proved to be a fickle ally as the waters of the Euphrates River slowly but inexorably shifted to the west, further hastening the demise of Sumer by leaving the cities and their monuments stranded in the desert. Today, only mounds of crumbling brick fashioned from the rich alluvial soil show that a great civilization once flourished here.

The still imposing hulk of the ziggurat at Uruk bespeaks the power of the
most important city in Mesopotamia
in the fourth millennium BC. Occupied for 5,000 years, Uruk—which was
surrounded by a wall encompassing
988 acres—now stands some 12 miles
from the Euphrates that gave it life.

Perched nearly 200 feet above the Euphrates in northern Syria, the ruins of Jebel Aruda mark the site of one of a chain of administrative and trading centers that served the southern part of Mesopotamia. This Sumerian outpost may have sent downstream copper ore, semiprecious stones, timber, skins, animals, and other goods that were unavailable in the homeland to the south. Its walls suggest a threat, perhaps posed by the local inhabitants, that might have led the colonists to desert it around 3500 BC after only 100 to 150 years of occupation.

Rising from fields of rubble, the 50-foot-high, now-truncated ziggurat at Ur was built and rebuilt as many as seven times and reached a height of 80 feet. Originally encircled by branches of the Euphrates, Ur, home to 30,000, withered away in the fourth century BC as the river shifted its course to a point some 10 miles away.

A structure put up in the 1890s to protect American excavators from hostile tribesmen crowns the great ziggurat of Nippur, built by King Ur-Nammu around 2100 BC. Sumer's most important religious center, Nippur also once stood on the Euphrates; today the bulk of the river's water flows 40 miles to the west of the ruins.

MILESTONES ON THE ROAD TO CIVILIZATION

Sumerians viewed their own genesis in simple terms: In the beginning was Eridu. Here, in what was once a marshy landscape in southern Mesopotamia, where the traditions of Judaism, Christianity, and Islam locate humankind's first home—the primeval paradise of Eden—the Sumerian epic describes a far different kind of dwelling place. When the Sumerians looked back to the start of time, they saw not a garden but a city. Tales of the birth of the world appear on clay tablets dating from approximately 2000 BC: "A reed had not come forth. A tree had not been created. A house had not been made. A city had not been made. All the lands were sea. Then Eridu was made."

The ruins of Eridu still linger in the desolate landscape west of the Euphrates, 12 miles to the southwest of Ur. A silent place of low mounds and shifting sand dunes, it now goes by the Arabic name of Tell Abu Shahrain. Only one conspicuous monument remains to mark this site, a mud-brick Sumerian ziggurat, or temple tower, in pitifully dilapidated condition.

In 1946 the archaeologists Fuad Safar and Seton Lloyd, under the auspices of the Iraq Antiquities Directorate, launched the first major excavation of Eridu. Two things had excited the archaeologists' attention: one, the legend dating the city back to an era preceding the Flood of both the Sumerian and biblical tales; and, two,

This curious terracotta effigy of a nursing mother predates the ancient civilization of Sumer. Its lizardlike face is typical of figurines produced by the Ubaid people, ancestors of the Sumerians.

the derelict ziggurat. Eridu, in popular belief, had been the original Sumerian shrine, dedicated to the freshwater god Enki, who doubled as the god of wisdom.

Since ancient peoples the world over tended to rebuild their temples for generations on the same sacred land, Safar and Lloyd reasoned that the remains of other, earlier temples probably lay underneath the monument. Perhaps the buried strata would even stretch back to the time when people began to build settlements in the heartland of Sumer—back to what archaeologists call the Ubaid period, which commenced about 5900 BC and ended around 4000 BC. Better yet, the layers and their pottery fragments might not only reveal who the earliest Sumerians were but also offer clues to the mystery of where they had come from.

Once the city of Eridu had been a well-watered site on a fertile plain. By the 20th century, however, its productive fields had turned to barren mud flats baked by desert heat and whipped by wind-borne sand. When the Iraqi expedition arrived at the site with building materials for their base camp, they encountered utter desolation. "The flat-topped mound," Seton Lloyd wrote, "with the scanty remains of a ziggurat at one end, seemed partly obscured by long curtains of drifting sand trailing far out into the plain on the sides away from the prevailing wind. We had no illusions about the climatic difficulties in store for us: endemic dust storms alternating with spells of heavy rain."

Fairly early in the first season of digging, the archaeologists made a welcome discovery: Beneath the southern corner of the ziggurat lay the crumbling bricks of a prehistoric temple that was built on a raised platform. And beneath these ruins they found the remains of yet another temple—then another, and another, reaching far back into the past, through the dry days of Eridu's demise to the long ages when water ran in what is now desert and the marsh dwellers constructed their buildings of reeds, mud bricks, and clay. As the team dug deeper, down to layer six, they discovered fragments of distinctive pottery and collapsed altars containing traces of what appeared to be offerings.

"In examining Temple VI," Fuad Safar wrote, "it took little time to discover that, so far from being the earliest building on the site, it represented a shrine already many times destroyed and rebuilt." The excavators, impressed and excited by their findings, hastened to report that "these remarkable buildings dated then from the

A 10-inch-long model of a boat made of terra cotta, uncovered during their pioneering digs at Eridu by archaeologists Seton Lloyd and Fuad Safar, resembles some of the vessels used today by fishermen in southern Iraq. The tiny craft, dating to about 4000 BC, may be the oldest-known representation of a boat. The modern wooden mast replaces the original, which long ago rotted away.

Workers labor at the lower levels of the great temple mound at Eridu in a composite photograph that shows some of the many levels of occupation unearthed by archaeologists. The later, larger temples with massive brick walls are seen on top, the earlier, smaller ones beneath. The miniature shrine at bottom dates to before 5000 BC, proving Eridu was one of the oldest-known settlements in southern Mesopotamia.

time at which Eridu was still a prosperous and extensive settlement, and had doubtless provided a focus for the religious life of its primitive, marsh-dwelling community. And herein lay their primary significance; for their architecture showed a formal maturity hitherto unsuspected in the inhabitants of South Iraq during this earliest prehistoric phase." The unmistakable sense of continuity strongly suggested that the direct ancestors of the Sumerians of the third millennium BC had built these temples.

Great quantities of pottery at the site, including broken pieces of votive vessels, bore the familiar painted designs of the Ubaid people, now known to have dwelled in southern Mesopotamia in the sixth millennium and generally considered to be the first settlers in that area. But in 1946, when the Safar-Lloyd excavation began, no one knew exactly how far back in time the Ubaid culture extended. For all its antiquity, Eridu had not yet proved to be the oldest Ubaid site; still, it held great promise of shedding light on the early stages of urban development.

Among the debris uncovered by the diggers in each of the temples were the bones of fish and small animals, evidently the remains of offerings left by worshipers. Safar and Lloyd reached the sixth layer before stopping work for the season. But already they could see indications that the seventh temple's crumbled core also contained fish bones, and the conclusion seemed inevitable—the fish had to have been left for Enki, the god of fresh waters. Pleased with the way their work had gone, the diggers departed and wrote up their exploits for their superiors and the *Illustrated London News,* then a popular forum for archaeologists.

The start of the archaeologists' second season demonstrated vividly just how difficult conditions could be. Safar and Lloyd wrote afterward: "During the summer of 1947, the drifting sand, for which Tell Abu Shahrain is so justly famous, had completely filled the cavity created by the temple excavation during the previous winter and was once more piled in a great drift against the flank of the ziggurat. As a result, many tons of sand had again to be removed before the work at this point could be continued."

The team's twofold objective included examining the area west of the ziggurat mound—where surface traces of a very early prehistoric settlement had turned up—and digging through the flattened ruins of the seventh temple to explore even older shrines below. In the settlement area, the excavators almost immediately uncovered

a cemetery that, as the pottery buried there with the dead would confirm, corresponded exactly in date to the sixth temple.

The cemetery contained an estimated 1,000 graves, of which the team excavated about 200 during the weeks that followed. For the first time, the scientists got a glimpse of the very people who had worshiped at the shrines: men, women, and children laid out on their backs, individually, in small tombs lined and covered with sun-dried mud bricks. They were only a collection of yellowed bones now, more than 6,000 years old, but these spoke poignantly of the people to whom they had belonged. In several instances single graves had been reopened in order to accommodate a second occupant, possibly a spouse. In addition to pottery—exquisitely painted jars, cups, dishes—the tombs contained personal belongings, even desiccated fragments of food suggesting sustenance for a journey to the afterlife. "Sometimes a man even had the bones of his dog laid across his chest," Seton Lloyd observed, "with a meatbone near its mouth." One little boy lay alone with the skeleton of his dog, which had also been provided with a bone for a snack.

The placid but eerie sight moved Lloyd. "There they all were," the archaeologist wrote to his wife, "lying neatly and quietly with their feet all pointing one way: the people who painted the pottery and brought their fish as offerings to that little temple, brittle and rather chilly, but with their comforting household things laid beside them. I can never get over that feeling of being suddenly among them when you find the graves."

Work beneath the ziggurat continued apace. The ruins of the seventh temple yielded to those of an eighth and the eighth to a ninth. The ninth displayed similarities to the upper shrines but on a smaller and simpler scale. What really set it apart, though, was its pottery, a somewhat different type from the kind the archaeologists had so far encountered, suggesting to them a possible pre-Ubaid culture. (Later research would show, in fact, that it belonged to a very early phase of the Ubaid period.) Beneath this layer, the team discovered vestiges of still earlier temples, for a total of 12 superimposed shrines, a truly phenomenal discovery. The earliest of the shrines, the excavators determined, had been founded on a pristine dune of clean sand.

The magnificent relief above, crafted about 2500 BC of beaten copper and including two stags and a lion-headed eagle, probably formed the lintel above the door of a temple built by King Aanepade, early ruler of the celebrated city of Ur.

The work of a Ubaid sculptor, the simple but powerful 6,000-year-old terra-cotta statuette of a bull indicates that the Ubaid settlers of southern Mesopotamia were sophisticated farmers with herds of domesticated cattle.

The entire task took four seasons of prodigious effort. By then, Safar and Lloyd had gone from the culminating phase of the Ubaid period to its bare beginnings, in about 5900 BC. Truly, Eridu was old, and the shaft that penetrated to its heart demonstrated a sequence of occupation spanning a period of more than 2,000 years.

"Come, tell me how you live" Agatha Christie Mallowan always wanted to know, and she used this invitation as a title for an autobiographical book relating her adventures on digs with her archaeologist husband, M. E. L. "Max" Mallowan. It also expresses what archaeologists hope to learn through their scrutiny of bricks, tools, and ornaments. "And with picks and spades and baskets we find the answer," the famous mystery writer noted.

But Agatha Christie, more than most people, knew that bigger mysteries than the long-forgotten daily lives of men and women lie beneath the surface of Mesopotamia. Only by working backward through thousands of years of human occupation would the archaeologists ever hope to discover how and when the wandering hunter-gatherers of the region came to settle on the land and farm it or find out where and when Mesopotamia's first villages sprang up and its first cities began. The task would not prove easy, partly because of the building material the Sumerians and their ancestors used.

Stone has always been hard to find in these parts; thus the inhabitants built their temples and settlements of a readily available

resource, mud, molded into bricks, an impermanent substance that dissolved as the generations passed. Through the centuries, the building blocks of Sumer crumbled and blended into the soil, and early excavators found it difficult to distinguish architectural features from the almost identical earth around them. The task of archaeologists in such a land is literally to separate dust from dust.

From the top of the ziggurat at Ur, one can, even today, see Eridu across the desert to the southwest and a small mound called Tell al-Ubaid about four miles to the northwest. Perhaps that is how

H. R. Hall, working at Ur for the British Museum in 1919, first observed the tiny place that would give its name to southern Mesopotamia's most ubiquitous pottery style.

Arriving at Tell al-Ubaid, Hall noticed that the surface was littered with thousands of painted potsherds, as well as numerous fragments of stone and metal objects, all of which suggested that something interesting might be buried beneath the sand. Almost immediately after excavations began, he came upon the ruins of a small rectangular structure, apparently a temple platform, that could be dated to about 2500 BC.

Clearing sand and crumbled mud brick from the sides of the structure, Hall stumbled upon a wondrous hoard: corroding parts of copper reliefs and statuary; magnificent remnants of lions, eagles, stags, and bulls with inlaid eyes and tongues of red stone; clay flowers with colored petals; and fragments of wooden columns encrusted with red stone chips and mother-of-pearl. But equally important, Hall discovered a lower mound near the platform, strewn with flint tools and fragments of handcrafted painted pottery. These utensils and potsherds—of the same type later found in great quantities at Eridu by Safar and Lloyd—clearly predated the breathtaking artifacts from the nearby temple.

At this critical juncture, the funds for H. R. Hall's venture ran out. Not until 1922 did a joint British-American expedition, led by Sir Leonard Woolley, return to Ur and the branch camp at Tell al-Ubaid to follow up on Hall's dig. The provocative site of al-Ubaid topped Woolley's agenda. "We excavated the mound," the archaeologist wrote afterward, "and were somewhat taken aback to find how little work it required—everything lay quite close to the surface. Under a few inches of light dust mixed with potsherds there came a stratum not more than three feet thick composed of hard mud in which were quantities of sherds of painted ware, flint and obsidian tools, and bits of reed matting plastered with clay mixed with dung." And below that lay virgin earth—"clean water-laid soil"—deposited eons ago by floodwaters.

Mud, tools, painted pottery, woven reeds in plaster—all of these, it appeared, were signs of an early Sumerian village. "This was, in fact," Leonard Woolley noted, "an island of river silt which originally rose above the marshy plain and had been seized upon by immigrants who had erected on it their primitive hut dwellings of reeds plastered with clay."

A variety of animals march in relief across a large, handsome drinking trough (below)—carved from alabaster in late fourth-millennium BC Uruk—that also pictures a stable made of reeds. Virtually identical buildings of woven-reed matting are still used by people living in the marshes of southern Iraq, as shown in the modern photograph at left.

An exquisite statuette of a woman, carved in glowing alabaster, reveals the artisanship of one of Uruk's sculptors, who seems to have rendered the arms and legs slightly asymmetrical to energize the piece. The figure originally had a head, possibly made of a different material, that was set with a peg in a hole between the shoulders.

Here, Woolley believed, the earliest inhabitants of southern Mesopotamia had built reed houses around the fertile marshes of a drying delta in the plain between the rivers. The scanty remains of the Ubaid villagers' lives told Woolley a great deal about them: The cow dung mixed with the mud plaster of the houses spoke to him of domestic animals; hoes and sickles showed that the people who lived here worked the soil; and primitive hand mills indicated that the villagers ground the wheat and barley they grew for their bread. It was plain, from the relatively advanced degree of their technology, that these firstcomers were already farming when they arrived in southern Mesopotamia.

These people had also made simple but remarkably fine pottery decorated with beautiful designs in black paint and highly fired so that the clay took on a greenish hue. In subsequent excavations, at Ur and at Eridu, Leonard Woolley and other archaeologists would discover this same handsome pottery, suggesting that all three sites were contemporary. Scholars would date those finds to the Ubaid period. However, since archaeologists specializing in the Near East routinely classify groups of prehistoric Mesopotamian sites in accordance with a shared ceramic style, the Ubaid culture came to stand for much more than just tiny al-Ubaid and the painted pottery that had been found there—but where the culture had come from and how the people had acquired their skills as potters and farmers remained a mystery.

With ready access to river waters and the sea, the little settlement of al-Ubaid lay in the heart of southeastern Mesopotamia's most fertile belt, along the fringes of the once-extensive marshlands that separated the delta plain from the rivers' estuary. The inhabitants made the most of the three converging ecological zones around their community. Certainly, they fished. Almost certainly, they grew and domesticated the date palm in the well-drained soil of the river levees. The natural abundance could indeed be suggestive of paradise: fish, game, and fruit that burgeoned year after year. But more important to their long-term economy, the people cultivated cereal crops such as wheat and barley.

The Ubaid culture ultimately extended across all of southern Mesopotamia and beyond it. By its distinctive pottery style, the culture's influence can be traced along the eastern coast of today's Saudi Arabia, into northern Iraq, and from there across Syria to the Mediterranean Sea. At Tepe Gawra, near the modern Iraqi city of

Mosul, a team of American excavators found still more evidence of the culture's spread. They uncovered a complex of three temples grouped around a plaza whose plans bore a striking similarity to later Ubaid temples at Eridu. To some scholars, this suggests that sometime during the late Ubaid period southerners exercised control over this northern town.

The contemporaries of the settlers at al-Ubaid lived in villages and small towns. They erected monumental buildings—similar to the temples at Eridu—that looked like little more than larger, better-made versions of Ubaid-period houses. These temples, however, became focal points not only for the towns that grew up around them but for the surrounding countryside as well. Significantly, such buildings reflected, in brick and mortar, a nascent social hierarchy that would become ever more elaborate and rigid as the towns grew into full-fledged cities. The emergence of these cities—the world's first—is best exemplified by the work of a team of German excavators at the site of Uruk.

Uruk—the Erech of the Old Testament—lies some 35 miles to the northwest of al-Ubaid and Ur. "Look at it still today," wrote a Babylonian poet some 4,000 years ago in his version of the Gilgamesh epic, "the outer wall where the cornice runs, it shines with the brilliance of copper; and the inner wall, it has no equal. Touch the threshold, it is ancient. Climb upon the wall of Uruk; walk along it, I say; regard the foundation terrace and examine the building; is it not burnt brick and good?"

The German archaeologists looked upon Uruk in the first quarter of the 20th century and admired what the Babylonian poet had described so long ago; the imposing city wall ran more than five miles. They could identify the final version of the temple to the sky god An. In an adjacent area, the excavators found the so-called White Temple—perhaps also dedicated to the god An—dating to the latter part of the fourth millennium. The largely intact whitewashed walls revealed a floor plan that corresponded to Temples XI-VI at Eridu, which dated to the Ubaid period. But whereas the Eridu structures had been built on a low platform, the White Temple sat atop an artificial mountain 40 feet high, reaching upward toward the sky like a ladder between earth and heaven—an early ziggurat, the most distinctive form of Sumerian architecture.

Bearded but otherwise naked, a king or priest prays to his gods. The limestone statuette carved during the Uruk period (4000 to 3000 BC) is from southern Iraq and may have been an offering, with the nudity suggesting a religious rite.

Nearby lies Uruk's other great temple complex—still marked today by the ruins of its impressive ziggurat. For thousands of years the faithful worshiped Inanna, the goddess of love and war, at this site, which served as the religious focus of the city. Beneath Inanna's temple precinct, the Germans found more traces of fourth-millennium Uruk. They uncovered fragmentary remains of a series of very large religious—and perhaps administrative—buildings contemporary with the White Temple. Some of these structures' walls bore polychrome mosaic decorations never before seen in such profusion *(pages 78-79)*; different colored cones of baked clay—or, more rarely, stone—had been pressed into mud plaster to create geometric designs. Subsequent archaeological investigations found this unusual technique to be widespread in southern Mesopotamia—but only during the fourth millennium.

The team made a sounding—a narrow excavation focusing on depth rather than horizontal exposure—deep down through the core of the most ancient sector of Uruk. They dug through 18 continuous but identifiable levels of occupation until they reached virgin soil at a depth of about 60 feet. The lowest stratum contained sherds of Ubaid-style painted pottery; but in a higher level dating to about 3500 BC something rather different appeared—plain, unpainted

HISTORY READ FROM POTTERY

Archaeologists working in the Near East depend far more on the detritus that they uncover during an excavation, especially potsherds, than on works of art to help pinpoint what groups of ancient peoples lived at the site and when they lived there. By examining a fragment's shape and decoration, analyzing its clay, and observing how it was made and fired, the archaeologists can deduce what period it belonged to and which culture produced it. Pottery, in short, can tell of history before anyone could write.

Potsherds have been especially valuable in dating and identifying the successive cultures that rose and fell in Mesopotamia. By the early sixth millennium BC, pottery making had already become a trade, professional artisans shaping lovely vessels and frequently decorating them with lively designs. In the following millennium, the potters began to employ pottery wheels, producing more uniform vessels with thinner walls. Later, during the fourth millennium, faster-spinning wheels brought about an explosion of plain mass-produced wares.

The rough handmade vessel pictured below (1) lay in the remains of the Neolithic village at Jarmo discovered by archaeologist Robert J. Braidwood. It dates to about 6500 BC, when many vessels were still being carved from stone. Beside it is a somewhat later jar (2) found at Tell Hassuna. The jar's incised herringbone decoration represents an attempt at artistry, but the clay, only lightly fired, remained porous.

The plate with stags leaping (3) shows the sort of vivid decoration perfected by artisans of the Samarran culture, which flourished between 6300 and 5500 BC. Drill holes on either side of the break indicate that the piece was repaired in ancient times. The plate to its right (4) is an example of Halaf pottery, produced between 5700 and 5000 BC and characterized by striking geometric designs, bold colors, and a polychrome finish.

1   2   3   4

A two-chambered kiln, used by potters of the Hassuna culture in the sixth millennium BC, is the earliest kiln ever to be found. It has a firebox below and the remains of an upper domed level with holes in the floor where the items to be fired were placed.

pottery in large quantity. Here was the kind of find the archaeologists had been waiting for. However unprepossessing this ware may have been, it had been thrown on a potter's wheel; in other words, it had been shaped not by householders for their own immediate needs but by artisans—specialists—producing quantities of simple goods for use by great numbers of people.

The age of mass production had arrived, and with it, the division of labor. And thanks to a growing technology, no longer was it necessary for every individual in a settlement to devote his or her full time to growing, harvesting, and processing food. Now work evolved to take care of the emerging needs of those individuals who led more sedentary lives and the many who still farmed. Thus there came into existence not just potters, but merchants, builders, artists, and other specialists.

The German team also retrieved elegant sculpture, pieces expressing the aesthetic and religious aspirations of Uruk's people. Through trade, they had obtained stone and used it to carve vignettes of their daily lives. Among these pieces were several outstanding works, including a ritual alabaster vase about three feet tall *(page 80)*, sculpted in panels of low relief depicting a ceremony honoring the goddess Inanna; an alabaster statuette of a muscular, bearded male

Below are eight vessels that originated in Mesopotamia or along the region's borders. Some of them were discovered intact, while others had to be reassembled from potsherds. Arranged in chronological order, these vessels demonstrate the development of pottery from one era and culture to the next.

A black crescent design decorates the lovely plate to the left below (5) found at Ur and dating from around 4300 BC, the late Ubaid period. The jar with its curved spout (6), made by a potter of the Uruk period, exemplifies the change brought by the fast-spinning pottery wheel. Undecorated and utilitarian, it was created late in the fourth millennium BC when most of such ware was mass produced and pottery had largely ceased to be a medium of artistic expression.

The jar below (7) dates to 3000 BC and belongs to the late Uruk period. Discovered in the United Arab Emirates, it may have been produced for trade. The jar next to it (8), decorated in black and red paint, dates from 2800 BC and displays both human figures and geometric designs. The vessel is characteristic of the first part of the Early Dynastic period, so called because the Sumerian city-states in that era were being brought under the rule of dynastic kings.

5   6   7   8

with eyes of shell and pupils of lapis lazuli; and the face of a woman, in white marble, whose features were rendered with consummate sensitivity and skill.

Small cylinder seals, less than two inches long and carved in exquisite detail, bore ritual scenes, mythological tales, and episodes from everyday life. From finds such as these and the number and succession of elaborate buildings they turned up, the archaeologists digging at Uruk in the 1920s recognized that the city could only have come into existence through the common effort of multitudes of people contributing their own special skills.

The archaeologists also discovered something truly astounding that supported this hypothesis: 500 to 600 small clay tablets dating to 3300 BC, some intact and some fragmentary, imprinted with pictographs and symbols. The people of Uruk had taken another giant step toward civilization and devised a means of recording their administrative and business affairs: 200 to 300 years in advance of the Egyptians, the Sumerians had begun to write *(pages 76-77)*. Their tablets—many "signed" with a cylinder seal—contain lists of personnel and commodities, references to commerce and councils, and head counts of domestic herds. These clearly demonstrate the importance of fish, dates, and domestic animals to the economy of Uruk. (Ironically or not, this tremendous breakthrough in the field of human communication would remain the exclusive province of the bean counters for more than 500 years.)

The pictographs used on the tablets reveal small details of daily life in Uruk. Some show sheep, goats, pigs, cows, milk pails, and cereals. Clay tokens used to record transactions carry recognizable images for plows, nails, axes, throwing spears, temples, and human heads and feet. On scenes from cylinder-seal impressions, signs for boats and carts abound. Music must have wafted through the streets, as evidenced by symbols for the lute and the lyre. Taken together, these hundreds of pictorial documents represent an incomparable tome on life in the city of Uruk during the latter half of the fourth millennium.

Now that professional classes had come into existence, they had to be specifically identified in the records, and words for certain specialties emerged: *nag-gar* for artisan or carpenter; *sanga*, priest; *sab-gal*, chief herdsman; *simug-gal*, chief smith. Human-kind had taken another step forward.

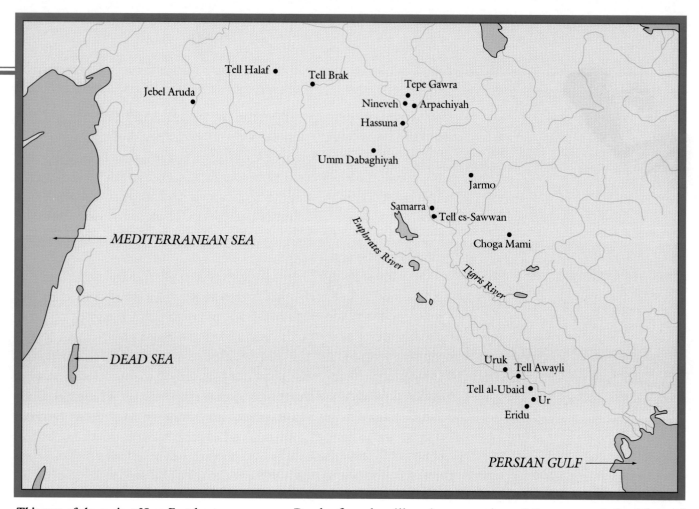

The following labels appear on the map:

Tell Halaf

Tell Brak

Jebel Aruda

Tepe Gawra

Nineveh • Arpachiyah

Hassuna

Umm Dabaghiyah

Jarmo

Samarra • Tell es-Sawwan

MEDITERRANEAN SEA

Choga Mami

Euphrates River

Tigris River

DEAD SEA

Uruk • Tell Awayli

Tell al-Ubaid • Ur

Eridu

PERSIAN GULF →

This map of the ancient Near East locates some of the prehistoric sites on the northern and the eastern borders of Mesopotamia described in the chapter. Here, in villages in the hills, lived the early farming peoples who may later have migrated into the Mesopotamian plain, where such settlements as Uruk, Ur, and Eridu evolved into the world's first cities.

Three staring eye idols are thought to depict a husband and a wife standing side by side, an official or priest with a high headdress, and a mother with her child in front of her. Thousands of these tiny figures have been found at Tell Brak, a distant outpost of Uruk culture in what is today's northern Syria.

By the fourth millennium, southern Mesopotamia had forged trade routes across almost the entire ancient Near East—from the Iranian plateau through northern Iraq into southern Turkey. Southern Mesopotamia's sphere of influence even stretched into Egypt, for art historians have identified motifs there that were seemingly borrowed from Mesopotamian cylinder seals.

In Syria, the Mesopotamian impact was more direct. The site of Tell Brak contains a southern-type structure, the Eye Temple—named for the thousands of so-called eye idols that were found in it. The sites of Jebel Aruda and Habuba Kabira-Tell Qannas look as though they were lifted whole from the plains of southern Mesopotamia and carried hundreds of miles to be set down on the banks of the Euphrates River in Syria. These were apparently colonies where southern merchants, perhaps from Uruk itself, engaged in the commerce of gathering such natural resources as timber and metals and then funneling them down the river to feed the ever-growing economy of the city.

The astonishing achievements of Uruk placed it well ahead of the region's other settlements. By the end of the fourth millennium, Uruk, at 250 acres, was at least twice as large as any other city. Eridu

had grown to perhaps 100 acres by about 3500 BC but shortly thereafter was largely abandoned. Ur remained little more than a small town. To the north of Uruk several sites, including Nippur, attained sizes of 100 acres or more. Although the Sumerians themselves regarded Eridu as the first city, archaeologists today would be inclined to award that particular title to Uruk, and only with the dawning of the third millennium would the rest of southern Mesopotamia finally catch up.

Although the little village of al-Ubaid and the settlement at Eridu could not match Uruk's grandeur, their importance to the search for the beginnings of Mesopotamian culture and of civilization in general cannot be overstated. Fuad Safar and Seton Lloyd's deep stratigraphic pit at Eridu—with the small one-room shrine the site's earliest inhabitants had built—raised as many questions as it answered. Where had those first settlers come from? Where had their forebears domesticated the plants and animals that these farmers brought with them as they entered southern Mesopotamia for the first time? To find the answers, archaeologists have looked away from the flat plains of the south toward the hills and steppe lands that lie to the north and the east.

A witty clay vase shaped like a porcupine with a bowl on its back, dating from the late sixth millennium BC, was found in the ruins of Arpachiyah, a prototypical Halaf village located on the northern rim of Mesopotamia.

Reginald Campbell-Thompson, a brilliant British archaeologist and a most economical man, was consumed with unearthing historical texts in cuneiform but had no great interest in prehistory. Campbell-Thompson's own incomparable finds at the archaeological site of Nineveh, on the outskirts of the northern Iraqi city of Mosul, revealed invaluable material about the life and wars of the first-millennium Assyrians and their kings. Yet C.T., as his colleagues called him, also knew of the extraordinary discoveries made in the south, at al-Ubaid in particular, that suggested a very early birth date for Sumer, and in 1931 he readily entrusted his younger colleague Max Mallowan with the task of digging a deep pit through the Assyrian remains in the Kuyunjik mound at Nineveh and down to virgin soil.

Mallowan and his wife, Agatha Christie, relished their extended Mesopotamian honeymoon, despite run-ins with C.T.'s parsimony. To work on her book of the moment, *Lord Edgware Dies,* Christie required a solid table, which she intended to buy—with her own money—at the bazaar. C.T. seemed

An aerial photograph of the mound at Arpachiyah shows the foundations of a round structure, or tholos, at the center. Most tholoi were small and served as houses for people of the Halaf culture of the sixth millennium BC. Scholars speculate, however, that the large ones of Arpachiyah, like this example, with its rectangular antechamber, were used for religious ceremonies. The largest tholos uncovered at the site had a 33-foot diameter and a 62-foot-long hall.

appalled by this unnecessary expenditure. Nobody at a dig had ever used anything but orange crates for furniture before. Christie made her purchase—for the unheard-of sum of 10 pounds. "I think it took him quite a fortnight to forgive me for this luxurious extravagance," she wrote in her autobiography; and even so she felt she had gone down a notch in his estimation.

Mallowan had problems of a larger order. C.T. counted on a quick dig, confident that Nineveh had been founded on a stone outcropping that lay about 40 feet down, after which they could go home. "Knowing how reluctant he was to spend money on a prehistoric excavation," Mallowan noted diplomatically in his memoirs, "I firmly encouraged him in this idea although I had my doubts."

Christie spun her web of mystery on her typewriter; Mallowan and his crew dug down and down through the Assyrian levels, then through those of the second, third, and fourth millennia. As the pit became deeper and more constricted, C.T.'s vexation grew. Mallowan's hunch had proved correct: They would have to descend to a very considerable depth in order to find the beginnings of life in Nineveh. Down at almost 70 feet, Mallowan uncovered a level of Ubaid pottery—evidence, as later scholars would point out, of Ubaid expansion to the north and possible dominance over previous cultures.

Campbell-Thompson fretted over the escalating cost to him in terms of manpower. Moreover, he had a fear of heights that made it pure torture for him to climb down to the bottom of the pit. Yet he was both a practical man and a brave one. It would be false economy—he allowed Mallowan to persuade him—to call off the operation before its goal had been reached; and as the senior archaeologist, he felt obliged to make the hair-raising trip down the steep dirt stairs once a day.

Mallowan relentlessly continued digging. Beneath the Ubaid layer he found what he later described as "a brilliant and gay pottery which we called Halaf ware." The name referred to a so-far little understood culture known to have existed in the north. The German archaeologist Baron Max von Oppenheim had been the first to come across this polychrome pottery at a place called Tell Halaf, near the source of the Khabur River. It was finely painted and fired, and its origins were unknown.

When investigations turned to the north in the beginning of the 1930s, this same pottery style cropped up at Arpachiyah and Tepe Gawra, not far from Nineveh. Following these finds, a newly reignited passion for investigation revealed that the culture characterized by the exquisite Halaf ware had come into being around 5700 BC—which archaeologists now know to be contemporary with the early Ubaid culture.

Surviving for some 700 years, the Halaf culture had extended westward from the foothills of the Zagros Mountains across northern Iraq and Syria to the Mediterranean Sea. The people lived in compact residences called tholoi—small round houses made of mud or brick, accommodating single families. Some of the tholoi had rectangular buildings attached, possibly for storage. The tools and

Skillfully carved by artisans of seventh-millennium BC Hassuna farming villages on the edge of Mesopotamia's hill country, a handsome alabaster bowl and a scoop with a bird's head handle glow with the beautiful veining of the stone.

Two plump female figurines of the Hassuna period, carved from alabaster, retain their original collars of blue beads. Hundreds of similar statuettes have been found in the cemetery of the village uncovered at Tell es-Sawwan, indicating that its farming people were rich enough to hire artisans to make burial offerings.

bones so important to archaeological interpretation showed that the Halaf people hunted wild animals but also raised domestic sheep, goats, cattle, pigs, and dogs—and cultivated crops.

The people also engaged in widespread trade with other settlements, as clay analysis of Halaf vessels found at various sites showed. At some time during the sixth millennium BC, the Halaf culture dwindled and died. What had happened to it? And from what roots had it sprung? These tantalizing questions, especially the second one, drove Mallowan in his dig at Nineveh.

Ninety feet down, where the shrinking dirt stairway reduced the working area of the shaft to about six feet square, Mallowan unearthed a handful of crude potsherds, 11 pieces in all, with an incised design never seen before. These small pieces of unknown pottery, which he called Ninevite I, at that time constituted the only relics of what appeared to be the earliest village dwellers of Mesopotamia. Not for a dozen years would more fragments turn up—in a more complete context—to help unravel the mystery.

Mallowan was gratified with his journey through time to the bottom of the deepest archaeological pit in western Asia. Campbell-Thompson breathed a sigh of relief that the costly dig had ended. Christie packed up her typewriter and worktable and prepared to move on to the next site. And Mallowan secretly tipped C.T.'s underpaid workers for every precious fragment found.

Investigations in the north continued. Fuad Safar and Seton Lloyd, who would later work together at Eridu from 1946 to 1949, ultimately tracked down the pre-Halaf culture whose relics Mallowan had first espied at the bottom of the shaft at Nineveh. In 1943 they set up camp at Hassuna, a small tell south of Mosul, where inspectors of the Iraq Antiquities Directorate had discovered Ninevite I pottery littering the surface, identical in type to the fragments Mallowan had found.

Safar and Lloyd faced the hardships and dangers inherent in any expedition to Mesopotamia. The two archaeologists were determined, however, not to surrender to such difficulties. "Our little tent camp at Hassuna tended to attract the nightly attention of Jabur tribesmen from the open Jazirah desert," Lloyd observed mildly. Camp morale sagged under the fre-

IN CHAFF AND BONES, THE TELLTALE SIGNS OF AN AGRICULTURAL REVOLUTION

It was quiet and gradual, consuming thousands of years, but it added up to the most profound revolution in human history. This was the great changeover by the Near East's Neolithic peoples from hunting and gathering to raising crops and taming animals—the sort of farming that made civilization possible.

The first step probably was the domestication of the wild sheep and goats that had roamed in the uplands between Mesopotamia and the Zagros Mountains of present-day Iran for untold millennia. Moving the animals in flocks from one pasture to another and fattening them on grains, the early farmers assured themselves of a handy supply of meat as well as milk and hides. Later came pigs, domesticated somehow from fierce wild boar, and then cattle tamed from aurochs.

The second step in this mo-mentous break with the nomadic past was the domestication of the grains that grew naturally in the same region, most notably barley and two hardy strains of wheat—emmer and einkorn. Culling the strongest plants from wild stands and sowing the seeds in small plots, the first farmers dramatically increased their food supply, made it more secure, and in good years produced a surplus that could be stored and even used for trade.

To trace how this revolution occurred and when and exactly where, archaeologists have enlisted the aid of zoologists and botanists who have analyzed long-buried animal bones along with the fragmentary remains of the ancient plants. At Jarmo and in the remains of other Neolithic villages, they have recovered carbonized wheat and barley kernels from sites of early fires. The size of the kernels and other differences tell botanists whether the plants producing them were wild or had mutated through domestication. Zoologists studying ancient bones have deduced that smaller ones indicate domesticated animals, which, over many centuries, became less hardy than their wild ancestors.

Archaeologists searching for the where and when of the great agricultural revolution have also studied pottery and figurines and other artifacts for the evidence they contain of the ancient interrelationship of animals and people. The magnificent bowl pictured below, with its lovingly detailed images of sheep, could only have been carved by an artisan living in a society with an already long history of tending tamed animals, growing crops, and depending on both for much of what made life possible.

Thick-wooled longhorn sheep move in procession around a handsome stone bowl that dates to the late fourth millennium BC. They look much like the sheep and goats of today's Near East seen in the background photograph on these pages, grazing a meadow below a rocky wall of the Zagros range.

In the artist's rendering at right, wild wheat (left) is compared to a spikier ear of its domesticated descendant, emmer wheat. The kernels of the wild variety broke off easily, thus making efficient harvesting difficult, whereas the more tightly packed emmer ears could be harvested with little loss of kernels. When sowing their fields, the early farmers apparently came to use more kernels with recessive genes from ears that did not fall apart when the stems were cut. This natural selection process led eventually to the emergence of emmer as the favored wheat grown by later Sumerians.

From the horns of ancient goats such as those below, specialists called osteoarchaeologists can determine the stages of the animals' domestication. The horn of a semidomesticated goat is almond shaped in cross section (gold outline), while the horn of a goat descended from generations of domesticates is flat on one side; that of a fully domesticated animal is kidney shaped. As their flocks of sheep and goats grew over the centuries, the farmers began keeping track of the animals with pictographs such as the image of a goat's head inscribed on a clay tablet (below, right)—and thus helped to give birth to writing.

quent exchanges of gunfire. "This was the situation when my wife joined me at Hassuna after our marriage in 1944. Our relations with the Jabur improved greatly when she set up a miniature medical clinic for their families."

Once they could work undisturbed by nightly hostilities, Safar and Lloyd found that the excavation far exceeded their expectations. During two seasons of digging more than 20 yards square, the archaeologists laid bare not only more pottery of the Ninevite I variety—which they renamed Hassuna for their site—but also evidence of several closely linked levels of occupation. Nearest to the surface, adobe houses and substantial buildings laid out in patterns clearly indicated a village quite similar to the 20th-century villages of the area; below that, more primitive dwelling places suggested farmyards. Near these had stood storehouses for grain, complete with husking trays for winnowing, flat stones for grinding flour, and clay ovens for baking bread. And scattered all about lay the tools of primitive agriculture and the bones of cattle, sheep, and asses.

The bottom most layer of Hassuna bore the carbonized scars of dead campfires that had warmed the site's earliest arrivals, surrounded by their rough-hewn possessions. The excavators turned up arrowheads, tools of stone and bone, clay pellets for use in slingshots, and crude pottery containers but not a trace of any form of man-made shelter or burial ground. In one place, a skeleton still lay in a crouched position beside the ashes of a fire that had also died some 8,000 years in the past. The simple nature of this campsite did not, however, disappoint the archaeologists—far from it. "Here then, as it seemed to us," Seton

Lloyd observed modestly, "were the symbols of a transition from the nomadic life of herdsmen and hunters to the economy of a settled farming community."

But the orderly chronology of cultures exposed by Mallowan's dig at Nineveh did not unfold so sequentially at Hassuna. Alongside the indigenous pottery, a much finer pottery with horizontal designs painted in brown began to appear in the upper levels of Tell Hassuna, as it would elsewhere at other sites of the Hassuna culture in northern Iraq. This new pottery—and the culture that it represented—was called Samarran because the evidence for it had first come to light in a prehistoric cemetery that was discovered beneath the medieval and modern city of Samarra.

The heartland of the Samarran culture lay south of Mosul, occupying a broad belt along the middle reaches of the Tigris River stretching west to the middle Euphrates in today's Syria and east into the Zagros. Most of the available information about the culture comes from two sites, Tell es-Sawwan and Choga Mami. Scholars now view the Samarran culture as a bridge, overlapping both the latter part of the Hassuna (roughly 6500-5500 BC) and the early part of the Halaf periods. Moreover, the latter phase of the Samarran is contemporary with the early Ubaid period in the south.

Although it has been plausibly suggested that the earliest settlers in lower Mesopotamia traveled south from the Samarran area, the nature of the relationship between the Samarran and early Ubaid cultures is not yet fully understood. Recent discoveries at a small Ubaid site near Uruk called Tell Awayli, however, have expanded that knowledge *(pages 68-69)*. As work continues, sites even earlier than Awayli may be discovered in southern Iraq, which could shed further light on the earliest settled communities and their relations with the rest of Mesopotamia.

The face of a flirtatious woman with appliqué eyes and nose, three painted beauty marks on each cheek, what seems to be a necklace of triangular beads, and a zigzag hairdo gazes from the neck of a jar crafted by Samarran potters of the sixth millennium BC.

Writing for the December 15, 1951, issue of the *London Illustrated News,* Robert J. Braidwood of the University of Chicago's Oriental Institute observed that the archaeological discoveries of the previous 20 years had tracked the evolution from village to town to first Sumerian city. "It still remained, however, to examine the very earliest stages of the farming, animal-breeding, and settled village community type of life in Iraq." In Braidwood's view, the sequence of prehistoric development discovered so far seemed to leap directly

CLUES TO THE ORIGIN OF SUMER

Nobody knows when the Sumerian civilization began, but detective work has shed tantalizing light on its origins. Seeking to unravel the mystery, Joan Oates of Cambridge University set out to investigate a suspected link between the Samarrans of northern Mesopotamia and the Ubaid people of the south, the Sumerians' direct ancestors. In 1968 she began a survey in a previously unexamined area of today's Iraq between the known limits of the Samarran and the earliest known Ubaid territories. Her team came upon a group of 8,000-year-old mounds. Excavation of the largest, Choga Mami, revealed an unknown level of Mesopotamian development in a layer dating to 5000 BC, situated below Ubaid remains and above four clear-cut levels of Samarran occupation.

It soon became apparent to Oates that there was something unusual about the layer. Examining potsherds from the site, she found them neither all Samarran nor Ubaid in style; they shared characteristics of both styles, pointing to cultural exchanges between the two peoples. The remains of irrigation ditches at Choga Mami further connected the Ubaid people with the Samarrans. The Samarrans were the first to develop irrigation on a significant scale. From the evidence of ancient canals near the mound, it was plain that the Ubaid settlers adopted this technology. But if the Ubaid people are the Sumerians' direct ancestors and were influenced by the Samarrans, then the Samarrans must be tied to the Sumerians, too. An unusually realistic Samarran clay head found at Choga Mami *(above)* would seem to suggest this: It has the exact same hairstyle as early Sumerian stone statues of 2,000 years later.

At Choga Mami the Samarrans constructed rectangular houses that, as these ruins show, abutted one another and consisted of two or three rows of small rooms each. They were often erected on top of or within the walls of earlier dwellings.

The archaeologists' tents stand on top of the Choga Mami mound (above). Nearby, contemporary villagers had dug an irrigation channel (above, right) that was little different from the Samarran canals of the sixth millennium BC. Small mounds marking the banks of a large, long-vanished Ubaid waterway are visible in the distance.

Digging down through the Ubaid occupation levels to the Samarran levels at Choga Mami, archaeologists found this potsherd decorated with sticklike dancing figures that combine stylistic elements of both cultures and demonstrate a link between the two. The finders designated it and other pieces like it as Choga Mami Transitional.

Further clues to the Sumerians' origins came from a southern site as well, the low mound of Tell Awayli. Believing this a prehistoric site, French archaeologist Jean-Louis Huot began excavating it in 1976. Pottery fragments found on the weathered surface dated to 5500 BC and revealed that the tell was at least contemporary with the oldest occupation level of the Sumerian city of Eridu. More surprisingly, the tell also contained potsherds—as well as the clay head above—from a Ubaid culture earlier than Eridu. Huot initially named this pottery Ubaid 0. He now associates it with Choga Mami Transitional. While not identical, the decorative motifs are similar enough to suggest communication between Tell Awayli and Choga Mami.

The buildings of Tell Awayli also indicated a Samarran influence. Excavating the mound's lowest level, the French team unearthed remnants of large houses similar in size and structure to those uncovered at the prototypical Samarran site, Tell es-Sawwan, in the north. But there was a crucial difference: The well-designed Awayli houses, ranging in size from 325 to 500 square feet, had columns (*below*). This was a surprisingly advanced feature, but more surprising, perhaps, was the fact that the Ubaid farmers of southern Mesopotamia should have lived in such sophisticated houses, rather than in the primitive huts that might have been expected.

The finds at Choga Mami and Tell Awayli push back the possible date of Sumerian origins 2,500 years. Unfortunately, the Persian Gulf War prevented work at Tell Awayli from continuing. Until both sites are reopened and more prehistoric sites uncovered, the mystery remains only partially solved.

Regarded as the most ancient house in southern Mesopotamia, this 7,500-year-old structure still displays the brick bases on which the wooden columns of a large central room once stood. As a further refinement, the walls were embellished with pilasters.

Mud walls of a granary dating from 4000 BC form a honeycomb pattern. The small storerooms, which were roofed over, protected the grain from moisture. The granary was only one of several uncovered on the same site.

The somewhat crude vessel at top right from Tell Awayli displays a geometric design similar to Samarran pottery. By contrast, the later bowl at right was made from a denser clay that yielded a finer product. Noteworthy is the criss-cross design painted on the bowl with glossy black paint.

from the most primitive form of hunting-gathering to the level of flourishing farming communities. There had to be something in between.

Braidwood argued that farming had originated much earlier than most scholars believed, and probably not on the alluvial plain of the south but in the rolling hills of northeastern Iraq where wild sheep and cattle, wild wheats and barley could be found. He sought to identify and excavate the earliest settled villages, always with an eye to this region. Only by finding a transitional site could he pinpoint the pivotal moment in time when nomads had ceased their wanderings and started to cultivate the soil.

In 1946, during a routine tour of northern Iraq, a staff member of the ever-alert Iraq Antiquities Directorate discovered such a site virtually by accident. He came upon a place called Qalat Jarmo in an area of rolling hills and valleys where stone chips littered the surface of a low mound near a still-occupied village. Local inhabitants denied knowledge of ancient relics in their own backyard, but the Iraqi archaeologist observed that a village sheik, in accepting a cigarette, used flint and steel to light it. The sheik conceded that the flint, and many others like it, had been found on the nearby mound. A close inspection of the flints revealed them to be products of the late Stone Age—strewn about in enormous quantities.

Braidwood checked out the site, a low mound covering about

Diggers labor on the 8,500-year-old site of Jarmo (above, left) where the archaeological team led by Robert Braidwood found indisputable evidence of early agriculture. Above is a well-worn stone palette probably used by the villagers to grind the wheat and barley they harvested. Dry farming began at least a millennium earlier in the green, well-watered foothills of the Zagros range seen in the photograph above, right.

three acres of a hilltop with a strategic view of the valleys below. At one time a stream had probably fed and watered those who lived nearby. A sounding in 1948 convinced Braidwood that this place contained the remains of a village older than any previously discovered in Iraq. Here, he thought, "one might expect to find the first signs of the transition from the cave-dwelling stage to that of the settled village community."

Two years later, Braidwood's team of archaeologists, botanists, zoologists, and geologists began a full-scale dig at Jarmo. The ancient village, occupying the space of a modern city block, consisted of about two dozen mud houses. Digging down through the heart of it, Braidwood found no fewer than 15 levels of continuous occupation spanning approximately 400 years. The top five levels revealed three-room dwellings with ovens and chimneys, bones of both domestic and wild animals, some clay figurines apparently representing

a fertile mother goddess, and numerous sherds from vessels that apparently had had elegant, sinuous profiles. Taken all together, the evidence uncovered at the site indicated that this had been a village inhabited year-round.

But in the layers below, Braidwood found a subtle difference. There were the little mud houses with their separate rooms, large stone tools, and smaller ones of obsidian and flint, pestles and mortars, animal bones, and the remains of barley, wheat, and peas, but no signs of the arrows used by hunters—nor of the storage vessels of fully settled people. Most significantly, he turned up no pottery—crude stone vessels, yes, but no pottery. Its very absence provided a clue, a nondiscovery to delight an archaeologist; here was the pre-pottery Neolithic village that Braidwood had hoped to find.

In the lowest levels, Braidwood and his team unearthed rough stone implements that appeared to be hoes, suggesting that the earliest people of Jarmo might have cultivated crops. The expedition's zoologists identified onager (wild ass) and gazelle bones in plenty and, among them, those of small but mature sheep and goats—the remains of domesticated animals *(pages 62-63)*. However, the most compelling indication that early Jarmo might be a missing link between hunting-gathering and primitive farming lay buried in the muddy clay of the huts. Snail shells and the hulls of acorns and pistachios, along with the evidence of wild animal bones, clearly indicated that hunting and gathering of wild foods provided much of the daily diet. But the presence in the same levels of cultivated forms of barley, wheat, and a variety of legume made it equally clear that the Jarmo villagers also grew some of their own food. Carbon-14 dating showed Jarmo's farming activities to have begun as early as 7000 BC.

For seekers of tangible treasure, the dig at Jarmo would have been a disheartening experience. For Braidwood, pursuing an idea, the excavation proved a triumph. He had found a settlement that was, as he put it, "on the threshold of a new way of life."

But the quest did not end at Jarmo. Diana Kirkbride, director of the British School of Archaeology in Iraq from 1970 to 1975, asserted that the hamlet of Hassuna—considered prototypical of the earliest stage of settlement in the northern plains of Iraq since its excavation by Safar and Lloyd—must have been preceded by communities in

Onagri race across the wall of an ancient building discovered at the late seventh-millennium BC settlement of Umm Dabaghiyah. An unusual village, it was inhabited only a portion of each year by hunters who trapped the wild asses in nets, then dried and stored the meat and skins. Below are an arrowhead and a flint blade, also from the same period; weapons such as these would have been used by the ancient hunters to kill and to cut up their prey.

regions of more abundant rainfall and more fertile soil. She hoped to search for such a spot in the foothills west of the Tigris.

Kirkbride, however, could not explore the region of her choice. Instead, she had to settle for a marginal area between true desert to the south and the more fertile steppe to the north. With the good-news/bad-news kind of luck that seems characteristic of scholars in Iraq, she found a pre-Hassuna village—from the same time frame as the latter part of the Jarmo sequence—called Umm Dabaghiyah on the very fringe of habitable land.

If agriculture had ever been possible in this dry, drab place, Kirkbride reasoned, it could only have been on a very small scale. The dig produced little evidence of the cereals that had been found in villages contemporary with Umm Dabaghiyah—only enough to suggest that these foods were not grown here but brought in from somewhere else. Stone tools at the site appeared more appropriate to a hunting than a farming community, although the permanence of the village did not jibe with a nomadic lifestyle. Putting these nuggets of information together, she concluded: "It is beginning to look as if it were a general period when small villages were being established for other than agricultural purposes in remote and ecologically unfavorable areas."

What possible reason could there be for people to live in such a forbidding place? As excavation proceeded, the answer to this question began to emerge. It seemed that the people of Umm Dabaghiyah presented a contradiction: Not nomads, but nonetheless hunters, they had built their settlement with scrupulous care. The village did not seem to have grown in the haphazard way that other settlements had. It actually appeared to have been laid out according to a plan and built to last. Although the domestic dwellings consisted of sandy clay and showed signs of frequent remodeling, two long shedlike structures, containing more than a hundred small and mostly unconnected rooms, were made of a tough amalgam of grasses and unusually fine clay.

To the modern eye, these chambers seemed to have something to do with the preparation and storage of a commodity. Wall paintings on some of the houses suggested what it might be; they depicted the chase and capture, with nets, of onagri. A thorough investigation of the structures revealed that a few of the chambers had drainage floors and that others, equipped with drying racks of a size to accommodate the skins of wild animals, and perhaps dried meat

and leather, served as storage rooms. Nearby lay huge quantities of animal bones, the vast majority of which belonged to the wild ass. "The entire village seems to have been specialized for hunting onager," Kirkbride observed. "However, there must have been more to it than simply killing and eating onagers."

From the telltale evidence of the dig, Kirkbride surmised that Umm Dabaghiyah had been a desert outpost or satellite community founded for the specific purpose of procuring various onager products, such as hides, hairs, and preserved meat, in quantities far greater than the few inhabitants could possibly use themselves. And Umm Dabaghiyah had probably not been the only home of these professional hunters. Their work at the onager pens was undoubtedly seasonal in nature. Indeed—Kirkbride theorized—they may have come from a larger community located somewhere to the north, a hometown to which they would return with their luxury items for local use or trade with other communities that specialized in altogether different luxuries.

If there had been such a home base, it has not yet been discovered. The push to find the first traces of Mesopotamia's earliest settled inhabitants has slackened since Kirkbride's expedition of the early 1970s, due to political conditions in Iraq.

Lingering, like dust in the desert air, is the thought that the city of Eridu was not, after all, so very old—nor, perhaps, was the myth surrounding the Garden of Eden. Each of these ancient locales, however, has served as a metaphorical touchstone for the great civilizations that followed them: Eden as the birthplace of humankind in Western culture and Eridu as the prelude for the glorious achievements of the Sumerians.

ECHOES OF URUK

A Sumerian legend tells of a race of monsters, half-human and half-fish, who introduced writing, agriculture, and metalworking to the inhabitants of Sumer's cities. The tale suggests that the Sumerians were as puzzled as some historians have been over why and how these giant leaps of civilization should have taken place in Sumer—an arid, treeless plain between the Tigris and the Euphrates rivers. Yet it was here, in this seemingly unpromising environment, that the world's first cities sprang up. At a time when much of the global population still sheltered in caves and crude huts and foraged for a living, Sumer's city dwellers were evolving a society with distinct classes ruled by a religious and political elite. Among other things, they learned to levy taxes and accept tribute, create large irrigation projects, and erect buildings of monumental splendor.

As improved agriculture led to surpluses of food and the accumulation of wealth, the need soon arose for recordkeeping, and this in turn inspired the invention of writing. Job specialization grew apace and spawned a class of professional craftspeople whose output would spur trade over surprisingly long distances.

These remarkable achievements did not happen overnight, however. Archaeological investigation has shown that Sumer's urban revolution took a couple of thousand years to unfold. But as the process developed, it presaged much that was to come, laying down the foundations for civilizations of the future. Art itself would advance, taking on a new realism as seen in the carving pictured above—from the great urban center of Uruk, the focus of this essay—in which a bearded figure guards cattle on a stone vase that was carved more than 5,000 years ago. Even early Sumerian literature, with its tales of heroes and natural calamities, would foreshadow great literary works to come, including some of the familiar tales of classical Greece and several stories of the Bible.

ECONOMICS, FATHER OF INVENTION

The greatest accomplishment of the prolific Sumerians was writing. Born of the need to account for stored or traded goods, the first examples appeared around 3300 BC and listed quantities of commodities such as grain, beer, and livestock. These and other items were deftly rendered by scribes as pictographs, simple representations of the things bartered, scratched on small clay tablets. As the system advanced, more complex ideas began to be expressed by combining signs such as a head and a bowl to represent the verb *to eat*.

Gradually, the pictographs grew stylized and abstract, although their meanings remained the same. New, blunter writing instruments fashioned from reeds or wood created wedge-shaped impressions known as cuneiform, after the Latin for "wedge." In time, standardized cuneiform signs came to represent not only things or ideas but also sounds, greatly enlarging the range of concepts that could be expressed.

Bullae, or clay balls, such as this one were used to record transactions. Participants would press tokens into a bulla's soft clay surface, then place them inside. In cases of dispute, the bulla could be opened and the tokens scrutinized. Scholars think this system contributed to the birth of writing.

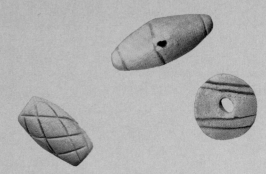

Small clay tokens such as the ones scattered here may have recorded business transactions or taxes before writing developed. It is thought that the shape of the token signified a specific item, while its size indicated quantity.

A clay tablet from Uruk, from around 3000 BC, illustrates the economic nature of early Sumerian writing. The pictographs represent the goods involved; quantities are expressed by the deeper holes and impressions.

A fragment of a seal from a jar found at Uruk demonstrates the pains Sumerians took to assert ownership. Such impressions were made by rolling personalized cylinder seals across wet clay—tablets, bullae, even flattened lumps affixed to baskets and closed doors. If the owner of such a unique item lost it, he had to announce publicly that it was missing to forestall others from misusing it. Most cylinder seals had holes through them so they could be worn.

One of the most beautiful Sumerian objects ever recovered, a marble cylinder seal from fourth-millennium Uruk portrays a bearded ruler feeding sheep flowering branches, perhaps symbolizing his role as benefactor of his people. Also shown are curving bundles of reeds representing Inanna, goddess of love and war, and tall footed vases used in temple rites. A reclining sheep tops the seal itself and serves as a handle.

77

The Sumerians were great builders, in spite of the limitations imposed upon them by their environment. Not only was the plain on which they erected their cities given to severe flooding, it lacked both trees and stone as well. But the inhabitants did not let this faze them: They boldly constructed their public and religious structures of sunbaked clay bricks. When inevitably these began to crumble after two or three generations, the people simply erected new buildings where the others had stood. At one of Uruk's sacred sites, archaeologists dug through no fewer than 18 levels of construction before reaching virgin soil.

To increase the durability of their edifices, the Sumerians expended remarkable energy in an effort to waterproof them. As these pictures show, one method was to face them with baked clay cones that had brightly painted heads— the world's first mosaics. Thousands of cones survive to this day, suggesting just how dazzling Uruk and other Sumerian cities must have been to the eye when the strong Near Eastern sun blazed down on their walls.

Pegs made of clay, with pieces of marble, shale, and limestone arranged in flower shapes at the head, served as facade ornaments during the Late Uruk period. This one turned up at Tell Brak, 750 miles upriver from Uruk itself.

Clay cones that once adorned a Uruk temple, their surfaces faded and patterns barely discernible, remain in place while the mud wall behind them has disintegrated. The cones, four inches long and a half-inch in diameter, were baked hard, colored, and driven into mud plaster in various geometric designs.

Hundreds of thousands of cones make up the fanciful zigzag, diamond, and chevron patterned mosaics adorning the remains of what may have been the first columns employed in monumental architecture. Later, seemingly without regard for the labor expended on them, these columns—from Uruk, but now in Berlin—were knocked down and a new temple complex built on the site.

Red, black, and white mosaics and the niches they embellished recall the traditional lifestyle of their builders' ancestral past. Niches, used to break up the monotony of Uruk's mud-brick walls, mimicked the look of early Mesopotamian reed buildings. The patterns formed by the mosaics may have been derived from woven mats and textiles used by the early inhabitants as wall hangings.

A WHOLE NEW WAY OF SEEING

This 5,000-year-old alabaster Warka vase, unearthed at Uruk, is divided into three parts, reflecting how the Sumerians thought about their world. Basic to existence are the water, crops, and sheep shown in the two bands at the bottom. Naked men occupy the next tier, carrying offerings (detail below). The top panel depicts the goddess Inanna accepting an offering. In a missing portion of the vase, the king stood in her presence, regally clothed. Plainly, in so hierarchically ordered a universe everyone knew his or her place.

During the heyday of Uruk, representational art came along quite rapidly, with Sumerian artists producing remarkably lifelike works that depicted human beings and animals in a variety of mythical and naturalistic scenes. Carved from stone and occasionally inlaid with shells and semiprecious gems, the pieces, like the ones that are reproduced on these two pages, exhibit the ancient artists' well-developed skills. Probably created at the behest of the rulers of Uruk, such artworks served as the furnishings and the embellishments for the city-state's most important buildings, including its temples.

This alabaster carving of a man with a muscular torso is rendered so realistically that it undoubtedly is the portrait of a specific individual, perhaps a king. Discovered in a jar buried beneath the wall of a 3100 BC Uruk temple, the seven-inch-tall fragment shows his hands clenched in what may be a gesture of worship.

Intended as religious offerings, these two miniature examples of Sumerian animal art, a cow and a calf, were among many such figurines unearthed in the precinct of the Temple of Inanna at Uruk. The calf has colored inlays, which are meant to mimic the creature's markings. Although live animals would certainly have been regularly sacrificed at the temple, the carvings functioned as permanent reminders of the donors' devotion to the goddess.

ROYAL SPLENDORS BURIED UNDER LAYERS OF TIME

This pendant, an eagle with lapis-lazuli wings and the gold head of a lion, ranks as one of Sumer's greatest treasures. Archaeologists unearthed it at Mari, some 280 miles up the Euphrates from the city of Ur.

The English archaeologist Sir Leonard Woolley and two of his colleagues alighted at a remote way station about halfway along the railway linking the Iraqi port of Basra with the capital city of Baghdad. It was a desolate spot, a halt in the middle of nowhere. To the east the nearest village was several miles away, the Euphrates River even farther. To the west lay desert, a forlorn tract of sand and mud flats punctuated by a few weathered hummocks. The foreigners' interest focused on the tallest of these, called by the Arabs Tell al-Muqayyar—or Mound of Pitch—because of all the bitumen fragments lying on the surface. The hillock had been explored in 1854 by J. E. Taylor, a British consular official at Basra, who discovered the ruins of a great ziggurat dating from Sumerian times. Taylor's excavations did little more than scratch the surface, but before he abandoned his quest he found inscriptions that identified the Mound of Pitch as the site of Ur, one of the world's most venerable cities.

For Woolley, appointed director in 1922 of an expedition organized jointly by the British Museum and the museum of the University of Pennsylvania, the ruined city was of extraordinary historical significance. Ur, he believed, was none other than the biblical "Ur of the Chaldees," described in Genesis as the birthplace of Abraham, patriarch of the Jews. A theology student who had once

contemplated following his clergyman father's footsteps, Woolley regarded the expedition to Ur as an opportunity to breathe new life into the Scriptures.

Woolley may have intentionally promoted his religious convictions to sway an American public fascinated by the prospect of seeing the Bible authenticated as history. Sometimes—as when he claimed to have uncovered evidence for the biblical flood—his enthusiasm for Old Testament references got in the way of the facts, but his few mistakes in interpreting the evidence only emphasized the general brilliance of his archaeological achievements at Ur. Over 12 arduous years, between 1922 and 1934, Woolley singlemindedly reconstructed a vivid portrait of a part of a long lost civilization as important and as fascinating as the Egypt of the pharaohs.

From prior excavations by others, Woolley knew that Ur had once been an important port left riverless by a subsequent shift in the course of the Euphrates, which now flows about 10 miles to the east. To establish the limits of the temple precinct walled in by the Babylonian ruler Nebuchadnezzar II in the sixth century BC, Woolley ordered two trial trenches dug along the likely course of the walls. When one of the ditches produced no evidence of any structure, Woolley ordered it to be deepened, and "at once," he reported, "things began to happen."

Buried at pre-Babylonian levels were clay and stone vessels, bronze tools, and beads and ornaments of gold, carnelian, and lapis lazuli. The last two materials, prized by Mesopotamian cultures as personal and religious adornments, must have been imported via long distant trade routes—carnelian from as far away as the Indus Valley, lapis lazuli from sources in eastern Iran. Clearly, Woolley had stumbled upon something significant, and from the nature and distribution of the finds, he was convinced that it was a cemetery.

A less meticulous man might have ordered a hasty and wholesale excavation, but to Woolley's eternal credit he immediately postponed work on the trench and transferred the crew to another part of the site. Concerns over pilferage at least partly dictated his decision, for he had noted that gold items only turned up when his

As seen in an aerial photograph, the royal cemetery of Ur and its tombs occupied but a small part of the site Sir Leonard Woolley excavated from 1922 to 1934. He also laid bare the remains of the ziggurat, the shrine and court of the moon god Nanna, and other religious and administrative structures the Sumerian rulers Ur-Nammu, Shulgi, and Amar-Sin rebuilt during the Third Dynasty of Ur, hundreds of years after the tombs were sealed. Later still is the enclosure wall; the Babylonian king Nebuchadnezzar II added it in the sixth century BC.

1 *Shrine of Nanna*
2 *Ziggurat*
3 *Court of Nanna*
4 *Temple and treasury*
5 *Residence of the high priestess*
6 *Palace of Ur-Nammu and Shulgi*
7 *Enclosure wall*
8 *Royal cemetery*
9 *Tombs of Shulgi and Amar-Sin*

foreman or other senior staff supervised the digging. Aware that the workers were selling valuable objects to local goldsmiths, Woolley came up with a plan to recover the finds. On Saturday, a payday, the archaeologist announced that he was offering a reward for every gold bead found in the dig. As he expected, the men greeted the announcement with dismay, for his reward amounted to about three times what the goldsmiths offered. While Woolley rested on Sunday, his workers hurried off to buy back the purloined items. Woolley was not in the least surprised when Monday's digging produced a veritable harvest of gold beads.

That was one problem solved, but as Woolley made clear, the lack of experience of the hired hands and archaeologists alike was the primary reason for postponing an excavation of the cemetery. "Our object was to get history," he wrote, "not to fill museum cases with miscellaneous curios, and history could not be got unless both we and our men were duly trained." In particular, Woolley knew he needed to work out a chronology of Ur's occupation that would enable him to fix the dates of the grave goods and establish them in their proper archaeological context. "The more rich the cemetery promised to be," he noted, "the more necessary was it to leave it alone until external evidence had given us a more or less definite chronology."

Over the next four years Woolley patiently constructed an outline of Ur's history, recording stratified levels of occupation that proved to span five millennia, from about 5500 BC, when the site was populated by prehistoric agriculturists, to about 400 BC, when the city was finally abandoned. By the start of the 1926-1927 season, Woolley had gained enough confidence in the skill and discipline of his team to start serious work on the cemetery.

In the interim, a new member had joined the expedition. In 1927 Leonard Woolley had married Katharine Keeling, who took an active part in the excavations, using her talent as an artist to illustrate the recovered objects. Always at Leonard's side, she was regarded with mixed feelings by the rest of the team. The widow of a British army officer who had committed suicide at the base of the Great Pyramid in Egypt soon after their honeymoon, Katharine possessed great charm when she chose to show it, but she was also snobbish, opinionated, demanding, and hypersensitive. She responded to any hint of opposition with anger and fell prey to every kind of illness—real or imaginary.

Leonard's assistant, Max Mallowan, was expected to act as

masseur to relieve the headaches that plagued her or to apply leeches to her forehead in a bloodletting treatment prescribed by a visiting doctor. She did not share a bedroom with her husband but none-theless demanded his instant attention if she awoke in the night needing treatment or comfort. Leonard, exhausted by long hours in the field and at his desk, slept through her calls, so a string was rigged from her bedside and attached to his toe. The Arab workers were terrified of her. Once, when a violent tribal quarrel broke out and could not be quelled by the other expedition members, the arrival of Katharine sufficed to cow the combatants into submission.

Leonard Woolley gently removes the earth from a votive figurine found at Ur. With equal patience and great ingenuity, he saved many other priceless items, including some that were so decayed and fragile they could be lifted only after being encased in wax.

Although Mallowan suffered as much as anyone from Katharine Woolley's overbearing ways, she did him an unwitting favor by ordering him to escort a lady visitor to Baghdad. The visitor was Agatha Christie, who had come to Iraq after the breakup of her first marriage. As she recorded in her autobiography, the ancient site cast a lasting spell on her. "I fell in love with Ur, with its beauty in the evenings, the ziggurat standing up, faintly shadowed, and that wide sea of sand with its lovely pale colours of apricot, rose, blue and mauve, changing every minute. I enjoyed the work-men, the foremen, the little basket boys, the pick men—the whole technique and life. The lure of the past came up to grab me. To see a dagger slowly appearing, with its gold glint, through the sand was romantic. The carefulness of lifting pots and objects from the soil filled me with a longing to be an archaeologist myself." Instead, she married Mallowan and later accompanied him during his excavations at the Assyrian capitals of Nineveh and Nimrud.

When work resumed on the cemetery in 1927, it soon became clear that the area contained two separate graveyards from different time periods. The upper one had been in use around 2350-2150 BC—the Akkadian era—while the lower was several centuries older, dating back to the latter part of Sumer's Early Dynastic period. Investiga-tions revealed that the older cemetery contained two types of graves: simple rectangular shafts for ordinary citizens, and more elaborate vaulted stone or brick chambers—indicative to Woolley of the resting

places of rulers and princes. In the ordinary graves, the bodies were laid as if asleep, either wrapped in matting or placed—together with jewelry and other personal possessions—in wooden or clay coffins or reed baskets. Outside the casket, the mourners had left offerings of food and drink, which suggested to Woolley that the Sumerians of ancient Ur believed in an afterlife.

Woolley's detailed descriptions of the grave furnishings belied the fact that most of the wood and matting items had disintegrated to little more than dust—"a film which a touch of the finger or even a breath obliterates more easily than it dislodges the plumage from the wing of a butterfly." In one tragic instance, Woolley watched the past vanish before his eyes. A worker had toppled an earth pillar, exposing on the stump what appeared to be the remains—actually no more than an imprint—of a wooden panel carved with figures. Since it was too fragile to remove, Woolley sent for a camera and began sketching the design. But he had hardly started when the heavens suddenly and unexpectedly opened. His men huddled around the treasure, trying to protect it with their cloaks, but their efforts were in vain; he could only lament as the images disappeared forever.

Katharine Woolley digs with her husband at Ur in 1928. Before the Woolleys' marriage the previous year, tourists gossiped about her being the lone woman in the camp. "Mrs. Keeling," wrote Leonard Woolley of his wife-to-be, "was at first very much hurt to think that her name could be so talked about. Perhaps that is still the price which women may have to pay for cooperation in scientific work."

Altogether, Woolley found 1,850 graves, of which he categorized 16 as royal tombs. With typical thoroughness, he plotted the position of all of them—rich and poor alike—with measuring tape and compass. "It was no mean feat," Mallowan recalled, "to take a reading in a high wind or a sandstorm when the needle waggled and spun to and fro like a ballet dancer." Woolley admitted that the painstaking and repetitive routine became wearisome—especially since more than half of the graves had been plundered or destroyed.

Woolley fixed his hopes on the grander structures, which he presumed to be royal tombs, only to discover time after time that treasure hunters had gotten there first, contaminating the archaeological record and leaving only a few scraps of gold leaf as evidence of the riches the tombs once contained. A tantalizing hint of that wealth turned up in the first royal tomb, which Woolley discovered at the end of the 1926-1927 season: The robbers had overlooked a

magnificent dagger. Fitted with a hilt of lapis lazuli studded with gold, a blade of burnished gold, and a sheath of solid gold carved in a plaited design, it was so deftly fashioned that one expert asserted it must have been made by Arab artisans in the 13th century AD.

The next season's excavations yielded even more dramatic discoveries. In another part of the cemetery, the diggers hit upon a trail of bodies that led to two adjacent tombs: one containing the body of a woman whose seal bore the name Queen Puabi, the other the grave of an unidentified man, who was presumably Puabi's royal husband. Outside the king's chamber unfolded an amazing scene of sacrificial carnage; the whole approach to the tomb was a veritable death pit, littered with the bodies of guards, attendants, and animals, along with fine objects *(pages 109-117)*.

Alas, the promise of even greater treasures inside the king's tomb was not to be fulfilled. Like so many others, it had been ransacked, and the researchers found no body and no treasure except for a gaming board and a silver model of a boat identical to those the Marsh Arabs of southern Iraq use to this very day. How the thieves gained access became clear when Woolley turned his attention to the adjacent tomb of Puabi.

It seems that Puabi had died after the king, and while digging the shaft for her tomb, the workers came upon the roof of the king's tomb chamber. Unable to resist the wealth they knew lay inside, they broke into it and stripped it almost bare, afterward trying to conceal their intrusion by covering the hole in the bottom of Puabi's death pit with a wooden chest that probably contained her clothes.

Puabi herself, the leading player in this lavish funereal drama, was found in a chamber that had been constructed beneath the floor of the death pit, alongside the looted tomb of her supposed husband. She lay on a wooden bier with her hands crossed. Two women—one at her feet, the other near her head—had attended her in death. Confirmation of her elevated rank was provided by a lapis-lazuli seal found above her chamber. It was inscribed with her name, Puabi, and her title, *nin,* or queen.

The style of the queen's headdress and jewelry was similar to that worn by the ladies found in both royal graves, but it was altogether more splendid. She had worn an elaborate cloak of precious metal and stone beads suspended on strings from a collar, and although the threads had disintegrated, Woolley was still able to trace the patterns running from her neck to her waist. Other personal

In 1929 Leonard Woolley (foreground, second from left) inspects the so-called Flood Pit, in which his workers uncovered an eight-foot-thick layer of water-deposited clay, devoid of artifacts, lying just above another level that was studded with pre-Sumerian objects. Woolley believed the clay was evidence of an inundation that drowned southern Mesopotamia and was perhaps remembered in the Old Testament account of Noah.

ornaments included huge gold earrings, a great gold comb, lapis and gold pins, amulets in the shape of animals, and 10 gold finger rings. Her headdress was her crowning glory. So large that it must have been worn over a wig, it was made up of coil upon coil of gold ribbon surmounted by three wreaths of gold rings and leaves. Beside her bier lay another headdress, consisting of a leather band adorned with gold animals and plants on a background of tiny lapis-lazuli beads.

In the 1928-1929 season of digging Woolley discovered another tomb of a royal personage, who may have been buried with even more splendid offerings, for though the chamber itself had been destroyed and its contents removed, its associated death pit—known as the great death pit—contained no fewer than 74 bodies. Of these, 64 were women dressed in ceremonial scarlet coats and laid out in neat rows, head to feet. The spectacle was amazing, recalled Mallowan; the victims appeared "to be like a golden carpet ornamented with the beech leaf headdresses of the ladies of the court, and overlaid by gold and silver harps and lyres which had played the funeral dirge to the end." Piece by piece the excavators put together a picture of a funerary ritual hitherto unknown and unimagined. Neither the literature of Babylon nor the eulogies of the Assyrian kings praising their Sumerian ancestors suggested that human sacrifice had been practiced in Sumer. It is true that a passage from the *Epic of Gilgamesh* speaks of a hero "accompanied in death by some of his retainers," but the exact meaning is not explicit.

Here, though, was proof positive that Sumerian rulers went to their graves accompanied by a host of subjects. Since both sexes were represented and the bodies were clearly of different ranks, Woolley guessed that the victims were members of the royal household, sacrificed to minister to their ruler's needs in another world. They had died with no signs of individual resistance—delicate headdresses all in place—suggesting that they met their fate with resignation, a state of mind possibly induced by some poison or soporific drug, such as hashish. This supposition is given weight by the presence of a cup beside each body.

Despite these revelations about early Sumerian funereal customs, many questions

"The filling-up of this building was done by degrees; clay was brought and trampled hard to make a floor over which offerings were spread and on which was laid the body of a human victim sacrificed in these later rites; earth buried these, and another floor was made and more offerings placed in order and another victim did honour to the dead below, and this went on till the top of the walls was nearly reached; then half of the building was roofed in with a vault of mud-brick, and in this subsidiary tomb was put the coffin of one whom we may suppose to have been the chief sacrifice. This chamber too was buried under the filling of the shaft, and probably on the top of it all there was erected on the ground-surface some kind of funerary chapel which should perpetuate the sanctity of the spot."

These reconstructions from a 1928 London Illustrated News *show the scene in the death pit moments before* (left) *and after* (right) *the sacrifice. Based on Leonard Woolley's actual plan of the excavation site, the renderings are, as he put it, "as faithful as may be."*

remained. As Woolley explained, "Generally the upper soil of the cemetery has been so disturbed by later interments and by tomb-robbers that for a long time we failed to find any evidence of the subsequent stages of the ceremony, but in the season 1928-29 we were more fortunate." While excavating an area containing many common graves, the archaeologists found that the shaft of one had been cut into a brick wall. Puzzled by this unusual arrangement, the men cleared a section of the wall, exposing a wooden coffin and some clay and alabaster vessels. There were also two daggers lying parallel to one another with a white cylinder seal between them, which bore the words *Meskalamdug the king.* These items had been carefully placed in a wooden box, the remains of which could be traced as gray lines in the soil. Apparently the box and its contents formed part of an elaborate burial ritual.

Excitedly the archaeologists turned their attention to the coffin. A man's body lay inside, but from the poverty of the goods that had accompanied him to the grave, he was clearly not royalty. Extending their investigation, the team discovered that the wall formed only one side of a subterranean building that contained other burials as well as food vessels arranged at different levels. Deeper and deeper the group dug, until at last they struck the roof of a stone vault that was characteristic of a royal tomb. Anticipation turned to dismay when it appeared that the chamber had been broken into. But further digging paid off, exposing the domed roof of a completely untouched royal tomb.

"It was particularly exciting," Woolley recalled, "because the top of the dome had been built over a centring [temporary wooden framework] supported by stout beams which ran right through the stonework, and the decay of these had left half a dozen holes in the roof through which one could glimpse parts of the dim interior and by the light of electric torches, could even see on the floor below the shapes of green copper vessels and catch an occasional glint of gold."

Inside lay five bodies—four of them men who, Woolley decided, had been sacrificed as part of the death rites of the fifth victim, a woman. Woolley was sure that she had been a queen, and certainly her attire suggested high rank, for she wore a golden headdress and the remains of her cloak were fastened by a golden pin. Beside her hand lay a fluted gold tumbler and a king's golden cylinder seal, which Woolley surmised to be some sort of token of farewell.

Bizarre and shocking as these rituals seem to modern sensi-

91

bility, the royal cemetery at Ur provides conclusive evidence that Sumer in the third millennium BC was a highly sophisticated urban civilization with a formally stratified society, artists and artisans capable of superlative work, merchants engaged in foreign trade, and well-organized armed forces.

Vivid glimpses of this distant world appear on one of Leonard Woolley's most important finds, the so-called Standard of Ur, discovered in an otherwise thoroughly plundered tomb. On one side, a king is depicted on the top row waiting to receive a group of naked and bound prisoners. Below, soldiers are shown marching in close order at the enemy, and beneath them are the royal chariots manned by javelin throwers. The reverse side contains scenes of peace and plenty, with the king and his nobles feasting and, below them, figures bringing in goats, fish, and other food supplies. Whether the Standard of Ur was commissioned to extol the fruits of peace or the spoils of war is unclear, but this tour de force may be taken as the defining image of the period—600 years of peace, war, and rivalry between the dozen or so city-states that emerged with startling rapidity in Sumer around 3000 BC.

The transformation of Mesopotamia from a land of scattered villages to a network of urban centers has been interpreted by some scholars as a response to natural alterations in the channel of the meandering Euphrates River. As certain areas lost access to the water necessary for irrigating crops, the population tended to concentrate in better-favored locales, giving rise to centers that were fortified to protect them from neighboring centers vying for the same resources of land and water. The concentration of a large population within the confines of a walled city brought its own tensions and conflicts, encouraging the development of new military, legal, and governmental institutions.

One thing is quite certain. Urban growth occurred astonishingly quickly in the case of Uruk. The most important city in Mesopotamia during the fourth millennium, Uruk grew in size fourfold almost overnight, increasing in area from about 250 to about 1,000 acres. It was probably the largest city in the world at that time. In the *Epic of Gilgamesh* the narrator boasts that Uruk occupied three square miles, of which one-third was city, one-third palm groves, and one-third brick pits.

IMPLEMENTS OF THE WORLD'S SECOND OLDEST PROFESSION

When people began settling in southern Mesopotamia in the sixth millennium BC, disputes must have arisen that may well have led to blood feuds and quick raids. But not until the fourth millennium, with the rise of cities that lay only 20 to 30 miles apart, did conflicts over the distribution of water rights, the boundaries of irrigable land, and other issues lead to larger-scale, more-organized violence. Warfare, civilization's ugly sibling, was born.

In order to fend off their attackers, the cities built massive walls, and over the course of the third millennium, standing armies became a permanent part of Sumer's social structure. One tablet speaks of 5,400 warriors who ate bread daily in the presence of Sargon of Akkad. But exactly how such big forces came into existence is unclear. Perhaps able-bodied men were obligated to fight according to a system of property ownership that is described in scattered early writings and reiterated later in the famous code of the Babylonian ruler Hammurabi. Known as *ilkum*, it offered subjects the right to hold land in exchange for a promise to serve the state—either by performing some benign task during peacetime, such as maintaining the canals, or by participating in a military campaign against a rival city-state.

Surprisingly, such struggles probably resulted in low death rates, scholars say, because the opposing forces were almost always evenly matched. Not only did they worship the same gods and share the same ways of life, but they also had similar military structures. Whenever an army fielded a new technology—especially one that was used for defensive purposes, such as the body armor or copper helmets portrayed on the Standard of Ur and the Stele of the Vultures *(following pages)*—the other city-states quickly devised a countermeasure.

Victory depended not on the tools of war, but upon the discipline and courage of the troops who wielded the weapons. The side that kept its nerve usually prevailed, while those who broke and ran abandoned any hope they had of surviving the enemy's spear thrusts and ax blows and were trampled underfoot.

Sumerian warriors such as the ax-carrying soldier at left were likely preceded into combat by shock troops who rode in ass-drawn wooden battle wagons similar to this clay model of the fourth millennium BC. Although such carts must have been difficult to steer, they were fully integrated into the Sumerian military. The vehicles were the world's first chariots.

The spear-wielding infantrymen in the middle band of the 4,500-year-old Standard of Ur, pictured below, wear long cloaks that experts consider the world's first body armor. Made of leather and dotted with metal disks, the cloaks not only guarded against broadaxes and spears but also stopped arrows fired from simple bows. Both the infantry and the chariot-borne shock troops in the bottom row are equipped with hammered copper helmets, another Sumerian invention. The uniformity of the soldiers' armor and weapons suggests a centrally controlled and outfitted fighting force.

The artisans who turned out the 31-inch-long ceremonial spearhead shown above, dedicated around 2600 BC by a king of Kish, came up with a solution to the age-old problem of how best to affix the blade to a staff. Early bone and obsidian spearheads, wedged into the end of a wooden staff and secured with leather lashings, came loose with use or split the shaft upon impact. This one, made of copper, was evidently designed to fit a cavity in the end of a staff and was secured with four pegs or rivets.

Soldiers of Lagash depicted on a limestone stele known as the Stele of the Vultures—fragments of which are seen at right—mass in rows nine men wide and six men deep. The monument was erected by a ruler of Lagash in about 2450 BC to commemorate his victory over the city-state of Umma. In the scene carved on the fragment at upper right, vultures carry off the severed heads of fallen warriors.

In these brick pits, presumably, workers manufactured the distinctive bricks that characterize all the cities of this period. Rounded on the top like a loaf of bread and flat on the bottom, they are, in engineering terms, a thoroughly unsatisfactory design. Why they were adopted by a people who already knew how to make better, more regular-shaped bricks, is a mystery. It has been suggested that perhaps speed of production was so important in the burgeoning cities that the bricks were simply fired in the same shape as they were dug up by a spade.

As yet, not enough is known from excavations in Sumer to put together an adequate picture of the archetypal Sumerian city of the third millennium. But beyond the confines of the Sumerian heartland, to the east of modern-day Baghdad, archaeologists in the 1930s uncovered the remains of several cities that shed light on urban patterns in the Early Dynastic period. Between 1930 and 1936, a team from the Oriental Institute of the University of Chicago, led by Henri Frankfort, excavated several sites near the Diyala River, unearthing temples, palaces, private houses, tablets, and significant caches of statues.

Founded in 1929 by the Egyptologist James Henry Breasted, with funding from John D. Rockefeller, Jr., the Oriental Institute employed the latest scientific methods and provided the best available amenities for its fieldworkers—a lifestyle regarded as unnecessarily luxurious by more traditional Old World colleagues. In Palestine, a kite balloon was used to take detailed aerial photographs, and at Tell Asmar, 40 miles from Baghdad and 20 miles from the nearest settlement, the archaeologists could take advantage of a fully equipped photographic studio and laboratory.

But as expedition member Seton Lloyd insisted, the Chicago excavators in Iraq had no qualms about harnessing manual labor to new technology when circumstances demanded. At Khafajah, one of the Diyala sites, in order to recover the plan of an important Sumerian temple that had been reduced to mud-caked ruins only one or two bricks high, team leader Pinhas Delougaz determined that the only possible solution was to expose and define every brick that remained. First, the mud was chipped away by hand, then the debris was blown away by jets from portable cylinders of compressed air. After two seasons' labor, the team had unearthed all of the remaining walls, revealing the layout of a remarkable temple complex. So carefully did Delougaz expose the site that 5,000-year-old footprints of

CREATING A DICTIONARY FOR A LANGUAGE WRITTEN IN CLAY

A written language so complex that few inhabitants of Sumer—even royal ones—ever mastered it, Sumerian today is known by no more than 250 people. But a project at the museum of the University of Pennsylvania, a leader in archaeological research in Mesopotamia, may someday make Sumerian as accessible as Latin and ancient Greek.

Since 1976 a team headed by Åke Sjöberg has been striving to divine the marks on the museum's collection of 27,000 cuneiform tablets—one of the world's largest—in order to create the first Sumerian dictionary. Building on work Sjöberg began in 1949, the team assembled a file of more than one million cards. Each bore the transliteration of a cuneiform sign, its English translation, the sentence in which it appears, and its source. That data, now computerized, forms the basis of what will be an 18-volume dictionary, containing the various meanings of the cuneiform signs, though not the signs themselves.

The 248-page first volume, consisting of transliterations that begin with the letter *B,* was published in 1984. The second, the *A* volume, came off the presses in 1992, and it will be well into the 21st century before the last volume appears.

"We're not just putting together a collection of words that we already understand," explains team member Hermann Behrens. "We have to figure out what the words mean, and it's extremely hard. Basically we are in the quarry, and we are breaking out the stones."

The difficulty lies not only in the number of signs—800—but also in the multiple significations of each sign. For example, an image of a fish can refer, simply, to a fish. But since the Sumerian word for fish is *ku,* the fish sign is also used to convey the "ku" sound, and the meaning of that syllable depends upon the context in which it is used.

Until today, each scholar of Sumerian had to make his or her own way through this labyrinth of possibilities. Teachers would pass along their research to favored students, but Sumerologists still had to spend years assembling their own file-card lexicons before they could make sense of many of the inscriptions that came into their hands. Now, at last, help is on the way.

Sumerian signs for date palm, arrow, and fish (clockwise from top) surround original dictionary team members Darlene Loding, Erle Leichty, Hermann Behrens, and Åke Sjöberg (clockwise from bottom left), shown with fragments of clay tablets.

a herdsman and his sheep were clearly visible in the temple courtyard. Fortified by thick double walls, the complex occupied an oval site covering more than seven acres and boasted a huge courtyard, warehouses, and a sculptor's workshop. The temple shrine itself had long since vanished, but the platform on which it had been raised could be traced, together with a flight of steps leading up to it. This layout—central shrine on an elevated platform—was more or less standard in third millennium Sumer and shows how the design evolved from the original crude shrine at Eridu—dating from 2,500 years earlier—and the series of subsequent temples erected over it.

The platform would eventually develop into the lofty stacked tower called a ziggurat, but already by Early Dynastic times the temple architects were working on a monumental scale and ornamented the brickwork exterior of the shrine with recesses, columns, and buttresses. Inside, however, the shrine retained the same basic feature that had been found in prehistoric Eridu: a mud-brick table or altar for offerings to the god whose image must have occupied the niche behind the altar.

All around the compound at Khafajah lay scattered pieces of sculpture depicting mortals, including copper figures of nude males that may have been votive offerings to the temple gods. At Tell Asmar, 21 statues were found carefully buried—by the Sumerians who considered them holy objects—under a pavement beside the temple altar. Originally, the statues had stood in front of the altar to intercede with the gods on the worshipers' behalf (pages 150-151). One votive figure from a later

Fashioned from gold, wood, and translucent green alabaster, this votive figurine of a woman from Nippur turned up in the ruins of the temple to Inanna, goddess of love and war. The garment, worn draped over one shoulder, would have been made of wool.

period carries the explicit inscription: "May the statue, to which let my mistress turn her ear, speak my prayers."

But the Sumerian temple was more than a place of worship. The largest and most imposing civic building, it stood at the center of the city and embodied the entire community. The Sumerians believed that each city was the divine property of its patron deity—to whom it had been entrusted on the day of creation—and expressed this conviction by representing the city with the picture of an altar and the emblem of the city.

In the Khafajah complex, houses belonging to priests have been tentatively identified. But in addition to priests, priestesses, diviners, and snake charmers, Sumerian temples employed a large secular staff: artisans to maintain the fabric of the building, scribes and administrators to run the economic affairs of the temple, and fieldworkers to till its considerable landholdings. Some of these functions may have been carried out by live-in staff, possibly slaves, but many jobs would have been filled by ordinary citizens commuting to the temple or working at home or in craft shops.

It is not too difficult to envisage the residential areas of a 5,000-year-old Sumerian city: They resembled the older quarters of modern Near Eastern cities, with mud-brick one- and two-story houses built around a central courtyard, separated by narrow alleyways. Individual houses were probably occupied by family units—husband, wife, children, and sometimes close relatives or slaves—and it is possible that the residential areas were divided into self-contained quarters housing related families. Many questions remain to be answered, however, for archaeologists have done little work so far in excavating shops, craft quarters, markets, or buildings where a city's leaders met to decide civic affairs, although it can be assumed that these kinds of places must have existed.

Some scholars see in the epic literature of Sumer indications that the day-to-day running of the city was originally in the hands of a council of elders. The first among equals was the city ruler, who was possibly a member of the temple elite. In times of crisis, decisions were taken by a general assembly of all citizens. Not surprisingly, the legendary accounts record that the first task of this congress was to decide whether the city should go to war against a rival or sue for peace.

A panther symbolic of Inanna battles a serpent on this vessel fragment found in her temple at Nippur. Researchers think the piece, made of chlorite and inlaid with colored stones and mother-of-pearl, was produced around the 27th century BC in southern Iran and carried to Mesopotamia by traders or diplomats.

THE STAFF OF LIFE: WAS IT BREAD—OR BEER?

"Drinking beer, in a blissful mood, with joy in the heart and a happy liver." So goes what is probably the world's oldest drinking song, recorded for posterity on a clay tablet from the third millennium BC. The image above right, from a seal, is even older—about 4000 BC—and depicts two Sumerians sipping beer from a large vat. They are using bent straws to penetrate the layer of yeast foam and barley husks on the surface of the unfiltered brew.

Until recently, Sumerologists had only these written and

Portraying a banquet of around 2500 BC, this seal impression shows musicians (bottom) entertaining guests seated around a communal beer vessel with straws protruding from the top. The seal itself came from the Royal Tombs of Ur.

pictorial records of beer drinking to study. But laboratory analysis of 5,500-year-old residue scraped from grooves on the inside of a clay beer vessel has, according to University of Pennsylvania professor Patrick E. McGovern, provided "chemical substantiation of what were archaeological arguments before." The jar came from Godin Tepe, a Sumerian trading post in the Zagros Mountains where archaeologists also unearthed storerooms containing barley.

Clearly, beer constituted an essential part of Sumer's economy, culture, and religion. Indeed, the brewmaster's art was the only vocation placed under divine protection—and from not one but two goddesses. Such female guardianship was only proper since Sumerian

women played a predominant role in the industry, both as brewers and tavern keepers.

The fermenting of malted grain to make an intoxicating drink predates Sumer's rise by several millennia. Archaeologists have long debated whether barley and wheat were first domesticated primarily to bake bread or to brew beer. Archaeologist Robert Braidwood posed the rhetorical question, "Did man once live by beer alone?" Lost in the dust of prehistory, a definitive answer will never be known, but it is likely that the knowledge required to prepare these two staples of life developed hand in hand.

Most Sumerians probably used reed straws to bypass the flotsam in the beer jar, but royalty merited more elaborate drinking paraphernalia. In Queen Puabi's tomb at Ur, Leonard Woolley found her solid silver cup and elegant gold straw.

Lively creatures from Sumerian mythology feast and entertain in these two shell-and-lapis-inlaid panels from the large lyre found in Ur's Royal Tombs. Visible on the right side of the lower panel is a beer vessel, source of the merriment.

It may have been during a period of increasing strife among city-states that the first man bearing the title *lugal*—literally "big man"—came to rule in Sumer. Perhaps the lugal was elected to command only for the duration of hostilities, but once he had command of the army, it was perhaps inevitable that he would eventually take complete control of the city-state and ultimately make his position a hereditary institution.

Almost certainly that is the process by which kingship came to Sumer—although Sumerian literature states that it first "came down from heaven," a claim contained in the King List, which gives the names of Sumer's rulers from before the Flood to about 1800 BC. As history, the list is unreliable, being a mixture of fact, legend, and fantasy, attributing reigns of such incredible lengths to many of the earlier rulers that the first eight kings alone are credited with occupying the throne for a total of nearly a quarter of a million years.

But the list was never meant to be simply a record of dynasties; it also served as a propaganda document designed to show that, from the time when kingship appeared on earth, a particular city was given a divine mandate to rule over all the others. Some authorities originally believed that the list of names was entirely mythical, but in the 1950s a young German Sumerologist discovered in Baghdad a fragment of a vase bearing the name Enmebaragesi, a historical figure who appears in the King List as a ruler of Kish, in the northern part of the alluvial plain.

According to the list, Kish was the first city to hold sway over its neighbors after the Flood. If Kish was indeed the seat of a ruler whose power arose independently of any religious authority, then it should have contained a secular palace as well as a temple. And that is what the English archaeologist Ernest Mackay found during a 1920s excavation. Boasting a towered gateway, buttressed outer walls, and columned chambers, this residence shares with another large building at Kish the distinction of being the earliest known Mesopotamian palaces.

Although in some respects the Sumerian kings may have functioned independently of the temple authorities, the belief that the

cities belonged to the gods made the ruler foremost among the patron deity's servants. In this capacity, the king was charged with the sacred duty of maintaining and restoring the city's temples.

The monarch also took a central role in the ritual of the Sacred Marriage, designed to ensure the prosperity of the city and its people. The rite, attested in poetry at the beginning of the second millennium but probably practiced much earlier, apparently culminated in sexual intercourse between the king, representing the god Dumuzi—an early ruler elevated to divine status—and one of the temple priestesses, who played the role of Inanna, goddess of procreation. One of the texts details the preparations.

"On the day of no moon, at the New Year, on the day of the ritual, they laid out the bed for my lady. They purified the bed-straw with cedar essence, and laid it down for her bed. Beside it they arranged her bedspread. When the bedspread had joyfully improved the bed, my lady bathed for the pure loins, she bathed for the loins of the king, she bathed for the loins of Iddin-Dagan. Holy Inanna rubbed herself with soap, she sprinkled oil and cedar essence on the ground. The king went to the pure loins with head high, with head high he went to the loins of Inanna. Amausumgalanna [Dumuzi] shares the bed with her, in her pure loins he is entertained."

Some scholars, inferring a link between this mating ritual and the scenes of sacrifice at Ur, have suggested that the opulent burials were not those of kings and queens, but of substitute priests and priestesses sacrificed after celebrating their union. But if that were the case, Woolley pointed out, then the "bride" and "groom" almost certainly would have been buried together, not in separate chambers. Also, the bride would probably have been a young virgin, whereas Puabi was a mature woman of about 40.

A union of a different sort—a diplomatic marriage between Sumerian religion and politics—was celebrated in Nippur, located midway between Sumer in the south and Akkad in the north, and belonging to Enlil, leader of the gods. Although the city was never the seat of a ruling dynasty, it had a special religious status as the meeting place of the gods, and no ruler who aspired to the title king of Sumer and Akkad could make good his claim without controlling Nippur and maintaining and restoring its temples.

Here, according to one Sumerian myth, heaven and earth were separated by Enlil during the creation. It was at Nippur—the

In order to demonstrate the awesome power of Ningirsu, the protective god of the city-state of Lagash, the artist who produced this silver vase showed the deity as a lion-headed eagle clutching two lions by the tail. Believed to be as kind as he was wrathful, Ningirsu is depicted elsewhere on the vase with goats and oxen, symbols of bountiful goodness. A cuneiform inscription by the maker/donor, running around the rim, invites the god to use the vase for storing butter.

"bond of heaven and earth"—that Enlil took a pickax and with it made a hole in the ground from which humankind sprang. And it was here, by tradition, that the gods met to decide the fate of Sumer.

Since the 19th century, the city has been the focus of intensive excavations by American institutions, principally the museum of the University of Pennsylvania and the Oriental Institute of the University of Chicago. In the 1950s excavations unearthed three large temples: a massive Early Dynastic structure whose deity has not been identified, the Temple of Enlil next to the ziggurat, and the Temple of Inanna, Queen of Heaven.

Two hundred or more tablets inscribed with literary texts were recovered from Nippur. One of them, a love hymn of Inanna, describes her ritual marriage to the ruling monarch: "Going to the lad, my young husband. To my young husband, to whom I cling like the apple to the bough. O lad, my young husband, whom I so love. To whom I, Inanna, cleave like the date to the palm leaf. Whom I, the maiden Inanna, so love. My young husband to whom I cling like the grape to the stalk. Amausumgalanna, whom I so love."

In 1960 more evidence was recovered indicating the reverence in which the Queen of Heaven was held. Alerted by a shout from a workman, James Knudstad, a staff member who would later become director of the project, saw buried in the altar in the temple sanctuary the statue of a female votary. About six inches high, the figure differed remarkably from the usual Sumerian votive offerings. Most statues were made of limestone, while this figure was fashioned from translucent green alabaster, with a gold face mask over a wooden head. Too rare and costly to be used in solid castings, gold was often reserved for the important features and shaped over a wooden framework—which perhaps helps explain why no images of the temples' chief deities have come to light.

Another 24 statuettes were unearthed from the sanctuary of the Temple of Inanna. Approximately 4,500 years old, many of the figures have a timeless human appeal—an old woman with a double chin, a bearded man and his wife holding hands, a wide-eyed worshiper gazing up with almost comical fervor.

The most eloquent testimony to the Sumerians' essential humanity, however, is provided by the thousands of tablets that have been recovered from Nippur. Mainly excavated around the turn of the century, they deal with such universal concerns as schooling, discipline, natural sciences and mathematics, the law and medicine. The eminent American Sumerologist Samuel Noah Kramer made a special study of the Nippur tablets, publishing some of their texts in a book recording 39 "firsts" in human history—from the first case of "apple polishing" at school and the first instance of juvenile delinquency, to the first medical "handbook" and the first experiment in shade-tree gardening.

Parents may draw some consolation from the fact that the generation gap was as wide 4,000 years ago as it is today. Here is a passage from a dialogue that begins with a Sumerian scribe asking his unruly and truant son where he has been.

"I did not go anywhere."

"If you did not go anywhere, why do you idle about? Go to school, stand before your 'school father,' recite your assignment, open your schoolbag, write your tablet, let your 'big brother' write your new tablet for you. After you have finished your assignment and reported to your monitor, come to me, and do not wander about in the street. Come now, do you know what I said?"

After more in the same vein, the father launches into a bitter rebuke, calling his son "perverse" and saying that he is sick to death of the young man's complaining nature. "Your grumblings have put an end to me, you have brought me to the point of death."

It is not, the father continues, as if he forced his son to work in the fields like the other boys. No, all he asks is that the boy follow his father's profession as a scribe. Apparently it is his son's failure or refusal to accept this vocation that causes the father so much grief.

One has more sympathy for the boy after learning that the Sumerian academic curriculum regime was dour and repetitive—"long days indeed," as one graduate recalled, with

The slate fragment at right, inlaid with shells, reflects the bitter warfare by which the city of Kish came to exercise dominance over southern Mesopotamia. Discovered in 1924 in the audience hall of the palace, the plaque shows a ruler returning from a military campaign with two bound and naked prisoners of war.

Stylized lions grace the surface of this stone mace head from the 26th century BC. Its cuneiform message refers to one Mesalim, king of Kish, which to the Sumerians carried a meaning equivalent to king of the world. Both from this title and other inscriptions it is clear therefore that Mesalim ruled over much, if not all, of Sumer, yet for reasons unknown his name does not appear on the Sumerian King List, a document that purports to include all the rulers.

the ever-present risk of canings by teachers or "big brothers." There were ways, however, of deflecting the wrath of the school staff, as this particular graduate recalled in later years. As a student he had once had the misfortune to be caned by several members of the staff in a single day for misdemeanors ranging from talking in class to poor schoolwork.

In a bid to curry favor with one tormentor, the student asked his father to invite the teacher home, where they could soften him up with a good meal and a "bit extra salary." It seems that the soft-soap treatment worked, because the evening ended with the teacher praising the young man for his diligence in studies, which the instructor hoped would make his student leader of the other schoolboys.

Kramer's skill as a Sumerologist was severely tested in the 1940s by one particular tablet from Nippur—a clay rectangle only about the size of a picture postcard on which a Sumerian physician of the third millennium BC had recorded his favorite medical prescriptions. Recalling his struggle to decipher the text, Kramer said: "In the course of the past decade, I worked at the tablet repeatedly, but made relatively little progress."

Then in the spring of 1953, Kramer found a collaborator, Martin Levey, a young chemist, who had a doctorate in the history of science. "Once again," Kramer recalled, "I took the tablet from its cupboard, but this time it did not go back until it was at least tentatively translated." While Kramer worked on the Sumerian signs, words, and grammar, Levey applied his specialized knowledge of the

ancient chemical and technological processes to identify the materials used in the more than one dozen prescriptions inscribed on the tablet.

Sumerian doctors made practical use of common mineral, animal, and vegetable derivatives. Sodium chloride (salt) and potassium nitrate (saltpeter) featured in many of the prescriptions. Snake skin and turtle shell were among the more exotic ingredients. Most of the medicinals, however, were extracted from the seeds, bark, and gum of plants—cassia, myrtle, asafetida, thyme, willow, fig, date, and others. The remedies concocted from these ingredients were intended for either topical use or to be dissolved in wine or beer for internal consumption.

One prescription for a poultice reads: "Purify and grind to a powder a water-snake skin, add the plant, the root of myrtle, crushed alkali, powdered barley, the skin of the *kushippu* bird, then pour water, boil it, and let the water be run off. Bathe [the sick organ] in it, and rub oil over it."

Unfortunately, not only have some portions of the text resisted the efforts of the translators, but the physician neglected to say what diseases the remedies are for. How efficacious they were is open to considerable doubt, but at least they appear to have been formulated on more of a scientific rather than superstitious basis.

"Not one god or demon is mentioned anywhere throughout the text," Kramer remarked. "It is a startling and rather unexpected fact that this clay document, the oldest 'page' in medical history as yet uncovered, is completely free from the mystical and irrational elements which dominate Babylonian medicine of later days."

If Nippur was Sumer's holy city—and probably a major seat of learning—then Kish was probably the first city-state to unite much or all of Sumer, with the title king of Kish implying rule over the entire Sumerian world. It appears that at some point in the third millennium, Kish did exert a degree of hegemony, but lasting political union proved elusive.

Under its heroic leader Gilgamesh—a deified figure in Sumer by 2500 BC, whose exploits were chronicled and aggrandized centuries later in Babylonian literature—Uruk wrested power from Kish, only to lose it in turn to other competing dynasties. Around 2500 BC Lagash—about 35 miles northeast of Uruk—emerged as a major city-state under its ruler Eannatum, who signaled his para-

This five-inch-long bull, cast of bronze and inlaid with silver almost 4,500 years ago, attests to the early date at which works of technical sophistication and high artistry were being produced in southern Mesopotamia.

The limestone wall plaque at right commemorates the role played by Ur-Nanshe, king of Lagash, in the construction of a temple. At upper left, the ruler is shown carrying a basket of mud from which bricks will be made; seated on his throne at lower right, he celebrates the work's completion. The 4,600-year-old plaque would have been fixed to the wall by a piece of wood driven through the hole.

mount status by assuming the title king of Kish rather than merely king of Lagash. Neither Eannatum nor Lagash, however, is mentioned in the Sumerian King List.

Kish's one-time position as acknowledged overlord of the Sumerian city-states is attested by the events leading up to this shift of power. Lagash and its neighbor Umma had once been embroiled in a territorial dispute that Mesalim, king of a then all-powerful Kish, had arbitrated by redrawing the border between the two city-states and marking the frontier with a stone monument, or stele. The Ummaites, however, violated the treaty, removing the stele and occupying the disputed territory until King Eannatum drove them out. With his closest rival defeated, Eannatum extended his power throughout Sumer, winning victories over Uruk, Ur, Kish, Mari, and even centers in Iran.

To commemorate his conquests, Eannatum erected and dedicated a victory monument between Lagash and Umma. Called the Stele of the Vultures *(pages 94-95)* because it shows birds attacking the corpses of the fallen, it is one of history's earliest known diplomatic treaties. After detailing Eannatum's military achievements, the inscription sets out the tough peace terms imposed on the Ummaite ruler, who swore, "Never unto wide eternity will I violate the boundaries of Ningirsu [patron deity of Lagash], nor will I infringe upon their dikes [and] canals; nor will I rip out their steles. If I violate the boundaries, then may the *shushgal*-net of Enlil [used to capture prisoners], by which I [the Ummaite] have sworn, be hurled down on Umma from heaven."

Under the constant threat of internecine warfare, human rights and personal freedom for the average citizen suffered setbacks. The rulers of Lagash and other city-states were obliged to increase their power at the expense of the populace at large, seizing landholders' property and appropriating funds from the temples to pay for military ven-

tures. But in times of peace the ruling elite, far from moderating their revenue-raising activities, actually extended them, imposing taxes and levies on virtually every activity, from sheepshearing to perfume making. If a husband divorced his wife, he paid the ruler or monarch five shekels, and when a man died, officials turned up at the burial to grab a portion of the grave goods.

This was the situation that faced a man named Urukagina, who ascended to the throne of Lagash sometime after 2400 BC. The first known king to acknowledge that a ruler's responsibility extended to rich and poor alike, he is credited with a series of reforms designed to protect individual rights. To end economic exploitation, Urukagina got rid of the parasitical officials who preyed on boatmen, fishermen, and cattle farmers. He also reduced the number of taxmen and reestablished the rights and authority of the temples.

More than 500 years before the Babylonian ruler Hammurabi introduced a formal legal code based on the premise that "the strong should not wrong the weak," Urukagina pledged that "he would not deliver up the weak and the widowed to the powerful man." If, for example, a rich man wanted to buy a poor neighbor's house but refused to pay a fair price for it, then "the 'big man' must not take it out on the lowly man." But Urukagina's ideals proved no match for military might, and after a reign of less than a decade, he was overthrown by Lugalzaggesi, ruler of Lagash's old enemy Umma.

By strength of arms Lugalzaggesi extended his dominion over Sumer—and beyond. According to an inscription found at Nippur, "Enlil gave to Lugalzaggesi the kingship of the nation, put all the lands at his feet, and from east to west made them subject to him; then from the Lower Sea [the Persian Gulf], [along] the Tigris and Euphrates to the Upper Sea [the Mediterranean], he [Enlil] put their routes in good order for him. From east to west, Enlil permitted him no rival; under him the lands rested contentedly."

Those lofty claims, however, proved to be hollow. Like so many of his predecessors, King Lugalzaggesi enjoyed only a transitory success. In 2334 BC Lugalzaggesi was overthrown, and it was left to his conqueror, Sargon of Akkad, to mold the city-states of Mesopotamia into the world's first empire.

TALES FROM THE DEATH PITS

The Sumerian king's attendants went singing to their grave. Perhaps drugged, likely buoyed by a belief that they would enter a better world, they stepped down the ramp to the music of a gold and lapis lyre. In the procession were copper-helmeted soldiers, women with their hair bound in gold and silver ribbon, grooms at the heads of oxen wearing silver collars. In all, 63 members of the court descended into the 30-foot-deep open pit and took their places in front of the sealed brick and limestone chamber where the king's body lay. Each courtier carried a small clay or metal cup.

"Some kind of service must have taken place at the bottom of the shaft," wrote archaeologist Leonard Woolley, some 4,500 years later. "At least it is evident that the musicians played up to the last. Then each drank from the cup." Whether they brought the poison with them (if indeed poison was used) or dipped it from a common cauldron is unclear. In any case, it appears that they sank peacefully to the mat-covered floor.

"Then someone came down and killed the animals and perhaps arranged the drugged bodies, and when that was done earth was flung from above onto them, and the filling in of the grave shaft was begun."

This was how Woolley envisioned a monarch's funeral at Ur in the Early Dynastic period, around 2500 BC. He based the scenario on evidence found in the 16 royal tombs he excavated there between 1926 and 1931. The clues were many but fragmentary. Only two of the masonry burial vaults containing royal remains had escaped the plundering of ancient graverobbers. And in the royal retinues' earth-filled death pits where most of the archaeological finds were recovered, bone and wood had long since turned to dust, and precious metals lay like wads of discarded tinfoil. Only after heroic efforts of recovery and restoration could crushed artifacts such as the rearing lapis and gold ram with its delicate shell fleece (pictured above as found and as restored) begin to tell their terrible and poignant story.

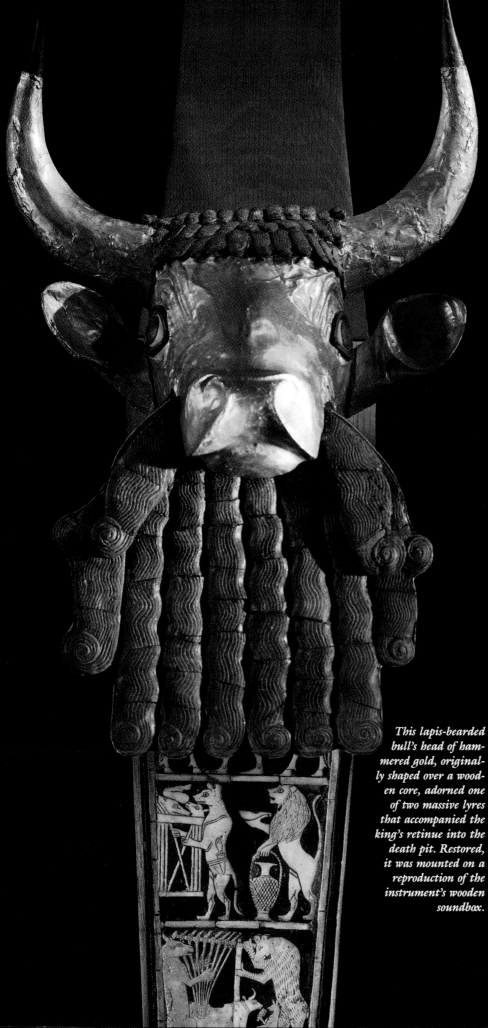

A FUNERAL'S LENGTHY LAST ACTS

The mass interment of the king's court was only the start of a lengthy rite that may have taken weeks to conclude. When the death pit was partially filled, a floor of beaten clay was laid over the dirt and a funeral feast set out. Fires were lit, libations poured, and animals sacrificed. Then more earth was shoveled in until it rose to about one story below ground level. There, a brick chamber was built to hold more royal retainers and offerings. Then the chamber was roofed and buried under a final layer of dirt.

Woolley speculated that an aboveground memorial marked the sacred site, noting wryly that "the tomb robbers who drove their shafts and tunnels with such accuracy underground must have been guided by something on the surface." Yet while the tomb chamber, once located, could be broken into and emptied with relative ease, the solidly filled death pits were another matter. "To get to their contents the whole pit had to be cleared out." That undertaking, he observed, "could not be attempted while any sanctity attached to the spot or any supervision over it was exercised by the authorities."

And so, from the moment that they fell from dying courtiers' hands, death-pit treasures such as the splendid bull's head at left lay unmolested. But in the vaulted tomb, plundered long ago, there was not so much as a seal to record the ruler's name. All that remained of his presence was a shallow depression made for his body in the earthen floor.

This lapis-bearded bull's head of hammered gold, originally shaped over a wooden core, adorned one of two massive lyres that accompanied the king's retinue into the death pit. Restored, it was mounted on a reproduction of the instrument's wooden soundbox.

Intent on gathering only items of intrinsic value, the thieves who plundered the king's tomb tossed this inlaid game board aside. Constructed of shell, bone, lapis lazuli, and red limestone, the board was hollow to allow for storage of the playing pieces. The game was evidently a version of a race game that was popular throughout the ancient world from the Mediterranean to India.

Holes mark the entrances to the Royal Tombs in the partially excavated cemetery site (right). Commented Woolley: "It is difficult to believe that out of this sorry looking quarry came such great treasure." One of the finds, the 26-inch-long silver model boat below was discovered wedged behind some loose stones in the king's tomb. Apparently the thieves who looted the site overlooked the fragile craft with its leaf-bladed paddles.

GLAMOUR THAT TRANSCENDS THE GRAVE

Next to the tomb chamber of the now nameless king whose burial is described on the foregoing pages, archaeologists found the resting place of a woman thought to be his wife, Queen Puabi. Identified by a cylinder seal from her tomb, Puabi went to her grave equipped to continue in the next world her glamourous, royal life.

Her tresses were laced and encircled by some 40 feet of gold ribbon and crowned by the spectacular confection of gold flowers, leaves, and ringlets below. She wore a cloak swagged across her bosom to her right shoulder, where it was ornamented by gold and lapis amulets *(above)*. She dripped with beads of silver, gold, red carnelian, and rich blue lapis—"astonishingly numerous," said Woolley.

Her toiletries included stibnite to darken her eyebrows, a purplish blue powder for her eyelids, tweezers, and a tiny earwax spoon. Twenty-three people accompanied the queen to the afterlife, one woman dying with hand still on her harp's strings.

Puabi apparently died years after her king; her pit was sited over his tomb. It was almost certainly gravediggers excavating for her death pit who broke into and robbed his tomb. They then placed the queen's wardrobe chest over the hole, where it hid their crime until Woolley uncovered it some 4,500 years later.

Many women in the royal cemetery had similar headdresses, but this diadem of Puabi's is the grandest. Its wreathes of gold beech and willow leaves studded with lapis and carnelian beads are topped by gold rosettes bowing over the queen's head. The huge hoop earrings were fashionable among Ur's rich ladies.

Depicting a feast, this impression was made by rolling onto wet clay a lapis cylinder seal that probably belonged to a member of Puabi's retinue who died in the pit. At the banquet, diners lift cups similar to the gold chalice at left, also from Puabi's tomb.

At the dig, Woolley shows off a remarkable piece of detective work. Finding gold fragments by a hole running down into the ground, he poured in plaster that hardened in a moldlike space left by the decaying wood of a harp. He displays the resulting plaster cast, which made possible the reconstruction at right.

NAGGING RIDDLES POSED BY A PRIVATE TOMB

One day workers uncovered what appeared to be a coffin embedded in the side of an excavation. Woolley wrote that the coffin "had decayed completely, but the impression of it in the soil was marvelously distinct, even the grain of the wood being, as it were, painted on the earth." When the foreman poked a knife into what looked like wood, the dust collapsed, and gold and lapis beads poured from the hole. With the treasure came a mystery.

For although the grave had the marks of a private burial—the body was in a wooden coffin and there was no death pit—it was, curiously, one of the richest at Ur, said Woolley, crammed with "objects found elsewhere only in royal graves." Among those in the coffin were two gold bowls and a gold lamp, each inscribed with the name Meskalamdug (but lacking a title, such as *lugal* for king); a double ax made from the gold and silver alloy electrum; a gold dagger with silver sheath hanging from a silver belt; and a beautiful gold helmet *(opposite)*. Outside the coffin were two more gold and silver daggers and vessels of gold, silver, and electrum.

Strangely, there was also a collection of costly women's jewelry.

The man, not yet 30, was no taller than five foot six, but "powerfully built." Was he a king buried like a commoner—or a private citizen with the riches of a monarch? A queen's nonroyal lover, perhaps, or a warrior heaped with wealth for his deeds? The mystery is further complicated by a seal found in an unnamed royal woman's grave. The seal is inscribed "Meskalamdug lugal"—King Meskalamdug. Woolley believed this was a different man. Others are not so sure.

Workmen pause while clearing earth from a stone dome that proved to cover a royal woman's tomb chamber. The horizontal line high on the earth face demarcates that lower grave from one above it. In the upper grave, diggers found the dagger below and the seal at lower right bearing the name of King Meskalamdug—put there, it is believed, in a tribute to the woman buried beneath.

This gold dagger and a similar one, as well as the seal at right, were buried in a wooden box in the upper grave, next to a man Woolley felt could not be King Meskalamdug—indeed, could not be a royal personage at all.

The glorious helmet of Meskalamdug—the likely commoner, not the king—is made of sheet gold hammered and chased to fit the contours of a Sumerian man's head, including his ears and his long hair rolled back into a bun.

Close inspection reveals that the vertical arrangement of cuneiform symbols on the gold bowl at right below is the same as one of the two columns of characters on the seal impression next to it. Both say "Meskalamdug." However, the clay impression, made with a cylinder seal found in a burial complex that included the tomb of a royal woman, also bears another cuneiform sign next to the name Meskalamdug. That symbol says "lugal," or king. The bowl does not bear the title lugal, one reason Woolley believed there were two different Meskalamdugs, a king and a commoner.

The horror attending the discovery of mass human sacrifice at Ur was tempered by a sense that the victims died willingly. "From the first, one could not but remark the peacefulness of the bodies," wrote Woolley. "There was no sign of violence, not even any disturbance of the delicate headdresses of the women."

To Woolley, the impression of calm implied that the rulers of the Early Dynastic period were regarded as divine or semidivine. "Quite possibly the word sacrifice in this connection is misleading," he ar-

gued, and those in the death pits died believing they "were going with their divine master to continue their service under new condi-

tions." He also allowed that a drug may have made them compliant.

Other scholars have speculated that the tombs were of priests, not royalty. Whatever the true story, the relics convey countless scenes of drama. In the so-called great death pit *(below)*, half the court ladies wore gold hair ribbons. From purplish oxides around the skulls of the others, Woolley deduced that they bound their hair in silver. Proof came with a touching discovery: a coil of silver ribbon near one body, apparently tucked inside an article of clothing that protected it from corrosion. It seemed that while the other young women had carefully dressed their hair for the ceremony, this tardy girl had hastily stuck her ribbon in her pocket, hoping not to be late for her own funeral.

Reins for a team of oxen threaded this double rein ring made of electrum and decorated with a gold ass. Found in Puabi's grave, the piece was once mounted atop a chariot shaft. Rich in relics, the great death pit (below) *contained 74 bodies but no royal chamber.*

Mosaic inlays and gold lions' heads decorate a modern reconstruction of the wooden land sledge they once adorned. The original was dragged into Queen Puabi's death pit by a pair of oxen; the four grooms who led the team were among the members of the queen's court who perished at her funeral.

THE BLOODY LEGACY OF THE GARDENER'S SON

May the lands lie peacefully in the meadows," ran the prayer of King Lugalzaggesi, the *ensi,* or ruler, of the city of Umma whose soldiers had made him Sumer's master. "May all mankind thrive like plants and herbs; may the sheepfolds of An increase; may the people of the Land look upon a fair earth; the good fortune which the gods have decreed for me, may they never alter; and unto eternity may I be the foremost shepherd."

The words survived on the scattered sherds of a broken vase, assembled by the American archaeologists who excavated the ruins of Nippur between 1889 and 1900, and the message, locked in the wedge-shaped indentations of cuneiform script, was heavy with historical irony. For the expedition already knew how the king's prayer had been answered and just what fortune the gods had granted him.

Lugalzaggesi, briefly lord of all Sumer, had clashed head-on with one of the ancient world's most extraordinary leaders, Sargon the Great, who ruled Akkad from his capital at Agade. Another Nippur inscription described Lugalzaggesi's fate with exultant brutality. "Sargon, the king of Agade, the King of the Land, laid waste the city Uruk, destroyed its wall; fought with the men of Uruk, conquered them; fought with Lugalzaggesi, the king of Uruk, took him prisoner and brought him in a neck-stock to [Nippur]."

With the coming of Sargon, the whole political dynamic of

Symbolically depicted as a bountiful provider, Gudea, pious ruler of Lagash, holds a vessel from which fish-filled water flows.

Mesopotamia changed irrevocably. The age of the independent city-states, warring among themselves for momentary supremacy, was over for a time. And although the dynasty Sargon forged would endure less than 200 years, his concept of a single authority to govern the disparate components of the world's first civilization would remain an aspiration to those who followed.

There would be long interludes without a clear central authority, even spells of anarchy. But 150 years after Sargon's death, a new imperium—and a reassertion of Sumerian political might—would spring from the city of Ur. Later, Babylonia and Assyria would emerge as Mesopotamian superpowers. All crumbled in time, but each had a successor. Sargon had many heirs. Few of them were his literal descendants, of course.

Unlike all those who had ruled Sumer since the beginning of its recorded history, Sargon was not Sumerian but Akkadian, a scion of one of the Semitic nomad tribes that had settled in the alluvial plain north of the Sumerians, perhaps during the fourth millennium BC. No great ethnic difference separated the great king from his subjects. *Semite* and *Semitic* are linguistic—not racial—terms used to describe a group of languages that today includes Arabic, Ethiopic, and Hebrew, distant relatives of the structurally similar Akkadian tongue that Sargon spoke. Indeed, apart from language, there seems little to distinguish the Akkadians from their Sumerian neighbors. The two peoples had lived together for centuries, sharing advanced agricultural techniques and city life alike; the earliest known Akkadian inscription, found at Ur, dates from about 2450 BC.

Then and later, Akkadian scribes used the readily available Sumerian script, which had been created to suit the entirely different Sumerian tongue—the equivalent of using Chinese ideograms to write Japanese sentences—causing a great deal of confusion to scholars ever since. It is sometimes hard to know in which spoken language an early tablet should be read: a cuneiform logogram could have the same meaning in both Sumerian and Akkadian, although it represented a totally different word. Probably many people in the third millennium—certainly among the educated scribe class—were bilingual, and some scholars maintain that Akkadian speakers dominated even before Sargon founded his dynasty. With the fusing of the whole Tigris-Euphrates basin into a single state, Akkadian replaced Sumerian as the language of administrative records.

Akkadian was used to record the deeds of Sargon, sometimes

Prisoners of war, their arms bound behind their backs, march to meet their fate in an Akkadian victory stele of carved diorite. Although Mesopotamian warriors killed and buried most of their opponents on the battlefield, they took some captive and kept them as slaves.

difficult to separate from the embellishments of generations of his admirers, for his reputation cast a long shadow. Myth and legend accumulated about him like a halo of cloud around the sun. More than 1,500 years after he died, he still generated passionate interest. A scribe in seventh-century BC Assyria left this supposedly first-person account of Sargon's origins: "My mother was a high priestess, my father I knew not. My mother, the high priestess, conceived me, in secret she bore me. She set me in a basket of rushes, with bitumen she sealed my lid. She cast me in the river that rose not over me."

It is impossible to know if such a Moses-like story circulated in Sargon's lifetime, but his humble origins are attested by other evidence—not least his name, or lack of it. Sargon—the form in which it has reached modern English via the Old Testament—represents the Akkadian Sharru Kinu, meaning "rightful or legitimate king," a description, rather than a name and one unlikely to be applied to a ruler who had come to power in an orthodox way.

Contemporary and near-contemporary sources, including the Sumerian King List, provide a brief chronicle of Sumer's rulers after "kingship had descended from heaven" until about 1950 BC. The list is often fanciful and always telegraphically concise: Before the coming of the Flood, it declares, a total of eight kings ruled for precisely 241,200 years, and few rulers receive more than an epithet or two. In Sargon's case, the King List describes him more fully as the son of a gardener, who rose to become cupbearer to one Ur-Zababa, king of Kish. The position probably equated to that of a senior administrator—someone close to the power of the throne—not a table servant. Even so, it was a long step away from the kingship that Sargon seized in about 2330 BC. Precisely how he accomplished his elevation remains a mystery.

According to later legend, Ur-Zababa had displeased the gods. Certainly, Lugalzaggesi of Uruk and Umma was on the rampage at the time, and Ur-Zababa could well have been one of his victims. Sargon may have usurped his defeated master, or he may have taken power of necessity in a time of war and chaos.

Scholars are much better informed about Sargon's subsequent career. In the temple of Nippur's chief god, Enlil, Sargon and his heirs erected both statues and steles to commemorate their triumphs and achievements. All have long since vanished; but they remained intact for a few centuries at least, and at some point for some inscrutable reason, a patient Mesopotamian scribe made an exact copy of all the inscriptions they carried. "Whoever destroys this inscription," read the wording on one monument, "may An destroy his name, may Enlil exterminate his seed." Despite the supplication to Sumer's gods of sky and air, the inscriptions were probably destroyed, but the anonymous transcriber's fragile clay tablet survived. Unearthed by Nippur's 19th-century excavators, it constitutes the nearest thing we have to Sargon's authorized biography.

It is a tale of adroit ruthlessness. In a lightning campaign after his enigmatic accession, Sargon marched to Uruk and destroyed Lugalzaggesi's armies as well as his city walls. Once the former overlord and "foremost shepherd" of Sumer had been captured and humiliated, Sargon took on the great Sumerian cities of Ur, Umma, and Lagash, where once more he "tore down the walls." From Lagash, a march of 150 miles brought his victorious army to the Persian Gulf, where he had his soldiers wash their weapons in the sea—a ceremony that unambiguously declared him to be the region's master.

From his new capital at Agade—somewhere close to Kish on the northern part of the alluvial plain—Sargon ruled an equally new Akkadian empire, a unified state in which Sumer's cities found themselves forcibly integrated. Conquered cities retained their original rulers but generally had a governor—backed by an Akkadian garrison—on hand to ensure continued fealty. In Agade, the king commanded what may have been the world's first standing army: "5,400 warriors ate bread daily before him," boasted one inscription. Certainly, he controlled a military force far more potent than anything

Garbed in a flounced dress, Enheduanna, daughter of the Akkadian ruler Sargon, performs a libation ceremony in honor of the moon god Nanna. A brilliant political strategist, Sargon appointed his daughter to the position of high priestess of Ur to ally his administration with the Sumerian religious hierarchy.

Sumer—or possibly the world—had seen. Carvings from the period of his dynasty show troops organized as fast-moving light infantry, many armed with bows—hitherto used primarily as hunting weapons. In conjuction with chariot-mounted shock troops, the foot soldiers demonstrated a long-range mobility indicative of highly skilled staff work *(pages 93-95)*.

The army, enlarged as necessary by part-time levies, allowed Sargon to extend his power far beyond southern Sumer. Campaigning northward along the Euphrates, he seized the city of Tuttul. There, according to his inscriptions, he "prostrated himself in prayer before [the god] Dagan" and, in return, "Dagan gave him the Upper Region: Mari, Iarmuti and Ebla as far as the Cedar Forest and the Silver Mountain." Mari was a Semitic city in eastern Syria, the Cedar Forest probably alluded to Lebanon, and the Silver Mountain meant the Taurus range, whence Mesopotamia obtained much of its silver, in southern Turkey. In the east, he defeated the combined forces of Elam—in present-day southwestern Iran—and made Susa, its principal city, a base for Akkadian power.

At home, the new capital of Agade became the radiant hub of the empire, receiving tribute from most of Sargon's realm. Trade boomed; according to Sargon's inscriptions, "he made the ships from Meluhha, the ships from Magan, the ships from Dilmun tie up alongside the quay of Agade." The names most likely refer, respectively, to the Indus Valley, Oman, and the island of Bahrain. Later legends sent his armies to these places, as well as central Anatolia (in present-day Turkey), the island of Crete, and an unknown "Tin Country."

In the ancient cities of Sumer, Sargon skillfully wove his authority into the fabric of religious traditions shared by Akkadian and Sumerian alike. Among the titles he claimed were those of "anointed priest of Anu"—the sky god, or An in Sumerian—and "great ensi of Enlil," the designation used by Sumerian city-state kings since time immemorial. His daughter, on whom he bestowed the Sumerian name Enheduanna, became the chief priestess of Ur's moon-god cult. She recorded the temple hymns and wrote

The obelisk of Manishtushu, a successor of Sargon, records his purchases of land in the area of Kish. In spite of its mundane subject, the monument is a masterpiece of artistic achievement, carved with elegance and precision, its inscriptions cut finely into the hard diorite. Manishtushu's title (left), *king of Kish, or king of the world, appears on the lower left-hand corner of each side of the obelisk.*

hymns to Inanna—and in impeccable Sumerian, too, not her native Akkadian—perhaps in an attempt to conciliate Sargon's resentful subjects. (Enheduanna became the first author in history to leave not only her works but her name to posterity. Sir Leonard Woolley's great Ur excavation even discovered her portrait—a limestone plaque that showed the priestess in the act of pouring a libation.)

Yet despite Sargon's soldiers and his canny association with Sumer's gods, discontent in his realm remained close to the surface. The city-states never reconciled themselves to Akkadian rule and chafed for their lost independence. When Sargon died—after more than half a century in power if the King List can be believed—his son Rimush faced an empire-wide rebellion. Ur, Lagash, and other cities rose against him, and he seems to have spent most of his nine years of kingship reconquering his father's domains. Apparently, he met a violent death; one cryptic text calls him the king "whom his servants killed with their tablets." The reference may be figurative—the power of the written word—or it could mean his courtiers literally stabbed him with the long pins on which they carried their cylinder seals. Whatever the circumstances of Rimush's demise, when the mantle passed to his brother Manishtushu, the pattern of revolt and repression repeated itself. Despite its outward splendor, the Akkadian empire never achieved an orderly succession.

About 2292 BC Manishtushu—according to the same baffling text, the king "whom his palace killed"—was replaced by Naram-Sin, Sargon's grandson and in many ways a reincarnation of the first Akkadian emperor. Like all of Sargon's heirs, he began his reign by crushing the inevitable revolts and then set out on a career of conquest that rivaled Sargon's own. He seems to have spent most of his 36 ruling years campaigning on or beyond the frontiers of Mesopotamia. Rock carvings in Kurdistan and southern Turkey mark the extent of his dominion toward the north and the east.

A stele, later carried away to Susa, shows the king trampling upon the corpses of his enemies, wearing the horned helmet Sumerian tradition reserved for the gods *(page 126)*. For unlike his grandfather, Naram-Sin had divine pretensions. In his inscriptions, his name regularly follows the star-shaped cuneiform symbol that indicated a god, and his preferred title was "the divine Naram-Sin,

A stele celebrating a victory of Akkadian king Naram-Sin, discovered in 1898, turned up in the Elamite capital of Susa, 200 miles to the east of where it was erected. The Elamites conquered the area in the 12th century BC and seized Mesopotamian works of art as spoils of war.

A rock carving in the Zagros Mountains (right), *believed by some scholars to portray a victorious Naram-Sin trampling his enemies, may have been commissioned by a later ruler in emulation of the revered victory stele above.*

the mighty, the god of Akkad, king of the four quarters." This assumption of divinity could be viewed as practical politics, rather than hubristic impiety. In Sumer, a city was considered the property of its resident god. By taking the god's title, Naram-Sin perhaps underscored his position as the sole authority in a centralized state.

As god-king, Naram-Sin was all powerful—the likely reason for the resentment and enmity he seems to have provoked. According to later chroniclers, Naram-Sin's assumption of divinity ultimately brought him disaster. The tale is told in an epic poem, *The Curse of Agade,* composed a few centuries after the Akkadian empire fell.

The poem begins as a hymn of praise to Agade in the days of its glory. The city was rich in both wealth and wisdom, its people prosperous and peaceful. Most of the known world brought its produce there. But Naram-Sin offended the god Enlil, and disastrous

retribution followed swiftly. While repressing a revolt in Nippur, the great king allowed his troops to sack the Ekur, Enlil's hallowed precinct, destroying its sacred groves until "the house lay prostrate like a dead youth." There was no limit to Naram-Sin's sacrilege: He cut grain at "the Gate of No Grain Cutting"; his men demolished "the Gate of Peace"; and they shamelessly carried the loot to his capital.

In this way, "the good sense of Agade turned to folly." Enlil swiftly took his revenge. From the mountains, he unleashed "a people which brooks no controls" until "it covered the earth like the locust." Soon, famine stalked a land where, because of brigandry, "the herald could not proceed on his journey; the sea-rider could not sail his boat." To soothe Enlil's anger, a group of lesser gods swore Agade would be destroyed: "Agade, you who dared assault the Ekur, who [defied] Enlil, may your groves be heaped up like dust. Your butchered sheep—may you butcher your children instead. Your poor—may they be forced to drown their precious children. Agade, may your palace built with joyful heart be turned into a depressing ruin." So it came to pass; the city was laid waste.

GIANT STEPS IN THE HISTORY OF ART

Glorify the king. That idea inspired Akkadian artisans to invent impressive styles and techniques to capture and project the power of their rulers. Indeed, art that portrayed monarchs as invincible became a potent propaganda tool during the transition from independent city-states to a unified kingdom in the third millennium BC. If commoners appeared at all in renderings of that era, they served merely as props for royalty.

Relying on minds even sharper than their copper and stone carving tools, the anonymous geniuses of the Akkadian empire learned to convey a sense of realism, previously lacking in Sumerian art. Whether sculpting sandstone steles taller than themselves or cylinder seals about the size of their thumbs, they imparted new sensibilities. They rendered musculature and facial features in much more lifelike fashion than their predecessors. And in order to heighten the drama of the kings' conquests, they pioneered the use of naturalistic landscapes as backgrounds in victory steles. Naram-Sin's stele, for example, shows the king—portrayed nearly one-third larger than the men—ascending a mountain using enemy soldiers as footholds *(right)*. There can be no mistaking Naram-Sin's divine kingship: He wears the horned crown reserved for deities, while the stars above his head represent the gods who have favored him with victory.

Either nature or, possibly, defacers erased much of the original inscription directly above Naram-Sin's head. Elamites, who looted the stele more than a thousand years after its creation, added their own inscription on the peak. Additional damage appears at the base and the top, where rays of at least one other star can be seen.

A three-quarters life-size bronze head uncovered in a trash heap at Nineveh may offer a closer look at Naram-Sin *(opposite, top)*. Archaeologists discounted initial thoughts that the head represented his grandfather Sargon because the craftsmanship so clearly eclipsed that found in earlier works. Even though the precious stones had been gouged out of the eye sockets and the nose mashed in a fall, the regal handsomeness persists. Yet it could well be that the portrait bears little resemblance to the king; Akkadian artists were probably the first to temper a quest for realism with a practical respect for their patron's vanity.

With the exception of a plummeting soldier, both the victors and the vanquished gaze up at Naram-Sin in his stele. By stressing the relationship between warriors and terrain, the single scene captures the flavor of war more effectively than earlier portrayals that depicted row upon row of stylized men ranged on flat land.

Framed by elaborately plaited hair and curled beard, the noble features of an Akkadian ruler—possibly those of Naram-Sin—continue to mesmerize viewers more than four millennia after an artisan created the hollow bronze casting. The realism of the lips, nostrils, cheeks, and eye sockets sets this work of art apart from earlier, cruder attempts at portraiture.

A cylinder seal of serpentine, dedicated to the fifth king of Akkad, leaves an impression in clay showing heroic figures serving water to buffalo. Seal makers apparently drilled details into the stone, then refined them with abrasives.

The Curse of Agade is a powerful story, graphic enough to eclipse the few solid historical facts from the period. There was indeed a barbarian people, the Gutians, who swept down from the mountains north and east of Mesopotamia, although they may have been more a symptom of problems within the Akkadian empire than the cause of its downfall. Naram-Sin was the last great king of his dynasty, but not the last of his line; his son, Sharkalisharri, reigned for an additional 25 years. Moreover, excavations of the Ekur temple at Nippur have found no trace of a great destruction during Naram-Sin's time. It may be that the king was ultimately the victim of skillful propaganda, his historical reputation "killed by the tablets."

Still, Sharkalisharri's plentiful surviving inscriptions go some way towards confirming the accusations of sacrilege directed against his father. The new king ostentatiously rebuilt the Ekur and made sure that his efforts received wide publicity. However, instead of Naram-Sin's godly designations, he contented himself with the unpretentious title of king of Agade.

But whether or not the father had offended the gods, the son saw little of their favor. His reign comprised one long struggle against internal revolt, frontier secession, and incursions by tribal peoples on the country's borders. Semitic Amorites from Syria, Lullubi from the Zagros Mountains, Hurrians, probably from northern Syria, as well as the predatory Gutians from Iran kept up the pressure, making it impossible to administer the creaking imperial state. When Sharkalisharri died, in about 2193 BC, the empire collapsed and anarchy reigned. "Who was king? Who was not king?" laments the King List. "The Gutian hordes" bore down upon the land. Agade crumbled and decayed. Its people were scattered; and even its location has so far eluded archaeologists' attempts at rediscovery.

Agade, if it is ever found, will make an immense addition to scholars' knowledge of the Akkadian period, a key missing piece from the much mutilated jigsaw puzzle of the past. However, the shape of the piece is already at least partly known. The relatively abundant inscriptions from Sargon's empire in their own way define areas where information is scarce.

Sometimes, though very rarely, an archaeological discovery yields not a piece that helps to fill a gap but a piece for which no gap exists, a piece so unexpected that the entire puzzle must be recast. In

the 1970s just such a revelation occurred and shook the world of Mesopotamian scholarship.

The story began in 1964, when the Italian archaeologist Paolo Matthiae started excavating at Tell Mardikh, about 35 miles south of Aleppo in Syria. Matthiae, an art historian and a Syrian specialist, had no specific purpose beyond the desire to expand the very limited current knowledge of life in ancient Syria. There were scores of possible starting points; mounds untouched for centuries lay scattered all over the country, and the nation's government, keen to establish a venerable pedigree for the modern Syrian state, expressed an enthusiastic willingness to help.

Matthiae chose Tell Mardikh because of its size—140 acres,

Rendered with remarkable realism, the bottom half of a girdled nude figure produced 4,000 years ago supports the remnant of a foundation peg, used in building rites, between its lifelike legs. Inscriptions on the base of the 350-pound hollow cast-copper piece proclaim Naram-Sin's nine battle victories in one year and his various construction accomplishments in the city of Agade.

A full moon and hidden spotlights dramatically illuminate the royal palace at Ebla. It was here that records on clay tablets were stored, many of which dealt with the textile industry for which Ebla was famous. The king alone kept 80,000 sheep for their wool, and well-watered fields around the city produced flax for linen.

including a central prominence the Italian team soon named the Acropolis—and its abundance of surface potsherds. Never before seriously excavated, the site had aroused expectations by the casual discovery a few years previously of a carved, ritual basin on the surface of the tell.

It was slow, unspectacular work; the digging season lasted only six weeks a year, and the unknown city whose ruins lay beneath the great mound was in no hurry to reveal its secrets. Nevertheless, by the late 1960s Matthiae and his team had unearthed several temples and a monumental gate, dating back to the second millennium BC. They had also dicovered their first inscription, on a headless basalt statue. His own modest knowledge of cuneiform notwithstanding, Matthiae's preliminary reading suggested that the statue was a votive offering to the powerful goddess Astarte made by a son of "the king of Ebla."

Scholars knew the name Ebla from the inscriptions of Sargon and Naram-Sin, who had claimed the city as a vassal and may have waged war against it, as well as a few references in ancient Egyptian records. But beyond that, no hard information had ever been discovered about the mysterious city-state, not even its location. Matthiae was convinced that he had found it.

Another Italian scholar, a Sumerologist named Giovanni Pettinato, was called in. No field archaeologist, Pettinato had spent his professional life immersed in ancient Semitic languages and their scripts. In Rome in 1969 he confirmed Matthiae's interpretation of the statue's message, and Matthiae happily assigned Pettinato the post of epigrapher to the expedition. But although the digging continued season after season, another five years passed before Pettinato's job had much more than an honorary significance.

During that time, the Italian expedition uncovered the remains of a third-millennium royal palace, with a clear destruction layer dated—based on pottery fragments—to the time of the Akkadian kings. It was probably the handiwork of Sargon or Naram-Sin. The Italians also came to realize the remarkable dimensions of ancient Ebla. In the city's heyday, around 2400 BC, as many as 30,000 people had lived within its ample walls. But no more inscriptions turned up, and there was still nothing for Pettinato to do.

Then, in August 1974, a telegram reached Pettinato from Syria; Matthiae had found 40 cuneiform tablets scattered on the floor of an excavated room in the palace area of the tell. Blackened by the

STIRRING VOICES OF THE PAST

Most cuneiform tablets contain either tedious mercantile inventories or mundane bureaucratic memoranda, but the Sumerians and Akkadians employed the written word in more creative ways as well. Below is a small sampling of their pithy proverbs, scorching imprecations, and whimsical humor.

Do not return evil to your adversary; maintain justice for your enemy, do good things, be kind all your days. What you say in haste you may regret later.

Making loans is as [easy] as making love, but repaying them is as hard as bearing a child.

Go up to the ancient ruin heaps and walk around; look at the skulls of the lowly and the great. Which belongs to someone who did evil and which to someone who did good?

A thing which has not occurred since time immemorial: a young woman broke wind in her husband's embrace.

Who has not supported a wife or child, his nose has not borne a leash.

Eat no fat and you will not have blood in your excrement.

Commit no crime, and fear [of your god] will not consume you.

Has she become pregnant without intercourse? Has she become fat without eating?

Bride, [as] you treat your mother-in-law, so will women [later] treat you.

If the beer mash is sour, how can the beer be sweet?

He who changes, neglects, transgresses, erases the words of this tablet, may the great gods of heaven and earth, who inhabit the world, all those that are named in this tablet, strike you down, look with disfavor upon you, may they chase you away from both shade and sunlight so that you cannot take refuge in a hidden corner, may food and drink forsake you, and hunger, want, famine, and pestilence never leave you, may the bellies of dogs and pigs be your burial place, let tar and pitch be your food, donkey urine your drink, naphtha your ointment, river rushes your covers, and evil spirits, demons, and lurkers select your houses [as their abode].

The gods alone live forever under the divine sun; but as for mankind, their days are numbered, all their activities will be nothing but wind.

fire that had destroyed the palace and half-baked by the heat, they still remained intact after more than 40 centuries.

An excited Pettinato flew straight to Damascus and reached the dig at 2:00 a.m. Despite the hour, he was immediately presented with the new finds. While Matthiae's team waited expectantly, the expert studied them. To everyone's exasperation, including his own, he made only a brief announcement: "I don't understand a word."

Since the days of Rawlinson and the other early Mesopotamian philologists, scholars had gained a working knowledge of several languages that employed cuneiform, among them Sumerian, Akkadian, Elamite, and Old Persian. As far as Pettinato could make out, the Tell Mardikh texts were written in none of them. Over the next few days, he managed to recognize a few Sumerian verb forms but could make no sense of any of the tablets. Clearly, the task of deciphering complete texts could not be accomplished in a few days on-site. Armed with photographs of the inscriptions, he returned to Rome and months of concentrated study.

By the following April, Pettinato had decided that the tablets were mostly written in a hitherto-unknown Semitic tongue, related to Akkadian but far from identical to it. The newly discovered language bore a distinct resemblance to later languages in the Syria-Palestine area, notably Hebrew, so he called the language Old Canaanite. Other academics viewed with skepticism the notion that cuneiform had been used by an indigenous Semitic people in Syria prior to 2000 BC. Pettinato would need more texts to convince them. Finding the texts would depend on the skills of Matthiae's team at Tell Mardikh—and luck.

Both were available, and in abundance. The next digging season brought the Italians an archaeological jackpot. Working steadily deeper in the palace area, Matthiae uncovered almost a thousand clay tablets amid the mud-brick walls that had collapsed during the great fire. Once more, the epigrapher hurried from Rome to Syria, in time to be present at one of the most momentous finds in the history of Near Eastern archaeology. He had just begun the task of transcribing the often-fragmentary texts—written in Sumerian as well as the baffling Old Canaanite—when one of Matthiae's archaeologists arrived breathless from the site. Beneath the ruined colonnades of the royal palace, he had found a chamber filled with yet more tablets, thousands upon thousands of them.

Although it was already evening, no one could wait until the

morning to evaluate the discovery. By the hissing light of kerosene lamps, Pettinato himself was lowered into the chamber. "I descended to a depth of eight meters," he recalled, "and, cautiously drawing near, I began to look through the first tablet that cropped out, half-covered by the sand of centuries." This time, he could read it clearly. It was a list of cities, mostly unknown, but again and again appeared the words *En-Ebla*—the king of Ebla.

The group worked all night, and by morning no one doubted

Clay tablets in Ebla's archives lie where they fell when their shelving collapsed in a fire some 40 centuries ago. An archaeological treasure trove, the tablets found at Ebla number more than four times all others unearthed from this period.

that they had broken into the royal archives of Ebla, containing almost 20,000 third-millennium tablets and fragments in all. There were even traces of the original wooden shelves where the records had been stacked by Ebla's archivists. The cache significantly increased the number of texts that a century of patient digging had so far revealed from the period before 2150 BC, and Matthiae's team was almost overwhelmed by the sheer magnitude of their discovery. For the next 10 days, they labored in shifts for 18 hours a day until the tablets had been safely removed and inventoried, with a careful record of their original position in the excavation.

But the cataloging was nothing compared to the work of transcription and decipherment. Although most of the tablets were only a few inches across, many carried more than a thousand lines of closely packed script, mostly in Old Canaanite—or Eblaite, as Pettinato, in deference to the misgivings of other scholars, decided to call the language he had been the first to recognize. Fortunately, the tablets included a collection of Sumerian-Eblaite vocabularies, and by the late 1970s enough of the texts had been understood to give a coherent picture of a remarkable civilization.

Most of the tablets contained administrative records, archive copies of the routine accounts of the city's daily business. A humdrum chore for the scribes who had prepared the records, some four millennia later they offered a complete cross section of a civilization whose very existence had been practically unknown. Before the Tell Mardikh discoveries, most Mesopotamian archaeologists had con-

Italian archaeologist Paolo Matthiae catalogs Eblaite pottery fragments under a protective sun shield. The numerous sherds unearthed at the site came from 14 levels of occupation and helped date Ebla, placing its peak around 2400 BC.

135

sidered third-millennium Syria of peripheral interest, if only because of the paucity of hard data. The new information made it clear that life in the ancient Near East had been richer and more complex than had previously been imagined.

The first surprise was the scale of the Ebla city-state. Although its exact frontiers remain obscure, one text claims a population of 260,000, of whom about 22,000 lived in the city itself. Ebla was run by 11,700 professional administrators—4,700 employed in four great palaces inside the city, with the rest scattered among outlying settlements and distant colonies. These officials controlled an advanced industrial economy dominated by the production and export of textiles and metals.

Ebla's goods found their way across most of the ancient Near East, notably to the great cities of northern Mesopotamia—Mari on the Upper Euphrates and Assur, future capital of Assyria, on the Tigris. Consignment and delivery notes reveal that Ebla's products reached as far afield as Anatolia in the north and Palestine in the south. Major shipments also went to Byblos on the Lebanese coast, probably for reexport to Egypt. (Egyptian hieroglyphic inscriptions were found on the floor of the palace in Ebla.) Some documents list more than 200 placenames, but most of their locations are unknown.

The stoic expression on this head from a diorite statue of Gudea, one of many he commissioned of himself, suggests the independent ruler's resolute strength. The whorls on his cap may be a stylized rendering of the tight curls of Persian lamb.

In Ebla, political relations went hand in hand with commerce. The state archives include copies of treaties negotiated with most of the city's neighbors, many of whom acknowledged Ebla's supremacy. But the city of Mari refused to acquiesce; it squeezed Ebla's trade routes, forcing a showdown which led to war.

A dispatch from an Eblaite general, Enna-Dagan, written in a unique style that Pettinato christened Military Bulletin, describes Ebla's response: "The city of Aburu and the city of Ilgi, which are in the territory of Belan, have I besieged and have defeated the king of Mari: heaps of corpses have I set up in the land of Labanan, heaps of corpses have I set up at Emar and Lalanium. Galalabi and the trading colony have I liberated. Iblul-Il, king of Mari and of Assur, have I defeated in Zakhiran and have set up seven heaps of corpses."

Filed near Enna-Dagan's after-action report, a memorandum records Ebla's profits from the campaign and their allocation: as a consequence of its defeat, Mari had to pay a tribute totaling 2,193 minas of silver, 134 minas and 26 shekels of gold. Fifteen percent went to the victorious general; Ebla's king received the rest. Like everything else in the merchant city, war had to pay its own way.

Ironically, it seems to have been the combination of wealth and military power that brought about Ebla's downfall. Strong enough to defeat Mari, it could not hope to confront the full might of the Akkadian empire, which saw the city's riches as an attraction and its power as no more than a nuisance. Ebla's destruction is generally dated to around 2275 BC, during the reign of Naram-Sin, although some argue for an earlier date during Sargon's time. Sargon claimed to have been given the city by Dagan, its principal god, and, if the king did not destroy it, he may well have exacted payoffs from its rulers. Naram-Sin likewise claimed the city for Agade. At the behest of one of these kings, Ebla burned, and the fire unleashed by the Akkadian soldiery sealed and baked the city's archives for posterity.

Seen from the remote distance of 4,000 years, the interlude following the fall of Ebla is a dark period, only dimly illuminated by anything resembling hard, historical facts. The Sumerian King List enumerates 21 rulers of "the Gutian hordes" during the course of approximately one century, but, in many cases, neither their names nor any account of their

A stone bull with a human's sublime countenance wears a horned crown, a declaration of its divinity. Dating from Gudea's reign, the figure has a small cavity in its back that probably held a container for votive offerings.

A FOUR-THOUSAND-YEAR-OLD PUZZLE

For more than 60 years, 89 pieces of carved limestone belonging to the 4,000-year-old Stele of Ur-Nammu were stored in the basement of the University of Pennsylvania's museum. In 1986 researcher Jeanny V. Canby began examining them, in an effort to reassemble parts of the ancient sculpture to which they belonged.

Discovered by Leonard Woolley in the shadow of the ziggurat of Ur, the monument had been smashed by invaders.

Yet despite its condition, he hailed the retrieved portions, with reliefs depicting Ur-Nammu's ceremonial activities, as a momentous find.

After the museum acquired the stele in 1926, a restorer rebuilt it from the larger sections as best he could but with little direction *(below, left)*. Years later, when a conservator began dismantling the nine-foot-tall work, she found that coat hangers, shoe strings, newspapers, and bits of crates had been used

as filler. The freed pieces, along with the other surviving fragments, were then compared and scrutinized—some scientifically. Drawings were made showing what is thought to have been their original arrangement, with blanks indicating missing segments that may never turn up.

A 1992 diagram of the front of the stele (below, right) *shows the partially reordered reliefs and the integration of some of the fragments not included in the original reconstruction* (below, left).

deeds have survived. Such brief reigns would seem to indicate chronic instability, although it is impossible to say just how much this instability affected those the Gutians presumed to rule. Judging by the few traces left from their occupation, the Gutians were probably quite few in number. The urban civilization between the rivers apparently remained largely intact. For most Mesopotamians, the Gutians more likely constituted a distant nuisance rather than a source of daily oppression.

Some Sumerian ensis certainly retained their independence during this interregnum. Around 2140, in the city-state of Lagash, on the fertile banks of the Tigris, one of them embarked on a vigorous program of reconstruction. Gudea—the name means "the one who is called to power"—built or rebuilt at least 15 temples in the town of Girsu, which had lain in ruins since the depredations of Lugalzaggesi centuries before. Little now survives of Gudea's efforts, except a number of statues of the ensi himself, carved with exquisite grace from polished black diorite, a hard, volcanic stone expressly selected as a symbol of permanence.

The statues' inscriptions explain how Gudea in a dream was commanded by the gods to do his pious work and describe the complex rites of purification and consecration that each temple required. They also tell how artisans and raw materials were brought from all over the Near East for the task: "From Elam came the Elamites, from Susa the Susians. Magan and Meluhha collected timber from their mountains, and Gudea brought them together in his town Girsu." Gudea's work demonstrates the enduring traditions of Sumerian piety and also indicates that southern Mesopotamia, even with the Gutians on the loose, was peaceful enough for large-scale construction projects that involved international trade.

Sumerian political power, too, underwent a revival at the ancient city of Uruk, located about 50 miles southwest of Lagash. Around 2120 BC Uruk produced a king called Utuhegal, who at last was strong enough to overthrow the Gutian overlordship. According to a near-contemporary narrative poem, he was "the king whose command no one can gainsay," and none other than the god Enlil instructed Utuhegal "to destroy the name of [the Gutian homeland], the snake and the scorpion of the mountain." With the help of allies from other southern cities, Tirigan, the last of the Gutian kings, was taken; Utuhegal "set his foot upon his neck" and "returned the kingship to Sumer."

A view of the northeast front of the ziggurat of Ur shows the restored central stairway of 100 steps leading to the first stage of the temple. During the Persian Gulf War in 1991, the Iraqis sheltered aircraft in Ur's sacred precinct and U.S. forces attacked the area. Fortunately, the ziggurat sustained only minor strafing damage.

A woman's plaintive expression was captured in alabaster by an artist of Ur around 2100 BC. The figure may portray the goddess Ningal, consort of the moon god Nanna, Ur's patron deity. Love songs endow Ningal with a passionate nature, and her earthly equivalents, the high priestesses, probably reenacted a sacred marriage ritual dedicated to Ningal within their temple precincts.

Utuhegal did not enjoy his triumph for long, but the circumstances surrounding his death, whether by accident or ill intention, remain a mystery. About 2112 BC Ur-Nammu, whom Utuhegal himself had appointed governor of Ur, ascended the throne. Under Ur-Nammu and his descendants, a new state flourished mightily in Sumer: the Third Dynasty of Ur—so-called because, according to the King List, it marked the third time the kingship was bestowed on Ur—or "Ur III" in the shorthand of archaeologists.

Like Gudea, Ur-Nammu was a great builder. Figurines of the period frequently show the king carrying building materials, and most of the 4,000-year-old foundation bricks that have survived still carry his name stamp. He constructed a massive new wall to enclose the 175 acres of his capital city; he dug canals for irrigation and communication; he built or rebuilt temples throughout his domain, including the Ekur at Nippur. Everywhere he built ziggurats that served as the focus of the temple complex in which a city's gods lived. His most grandiose construction—and the best preserved—was the great ziggurat of Ur, dedicated to the moon god Nanna.

The thorough investigation of Leonard Woolley has permitted the reconstruction of Ur-Nammu's ziggurat—at least on paper. With a solid core of mud bricks and a veneer of baked bricks, the tower was crowned by a small temple that would have stood on the uppermost stage. But all traces of this temple have long since disappeared. Slits in the exterior brickwork led deep into the tower's core. These enabled the potentially damaging moisture that accumulated inside the massive construction to evaporate harmlessly away.

Less tangible but no less important than his ziggurats was Ur-Nammu's rebuilding of Sumerian law. His legal code is older than any other so far recovered, though the Ebla archives may yet provide an earlier example. Although it has been preserved only in fragmentary form, its prologue, discovered at Nippur, speaks eloquently across the vast bridge of time: "Then did Ur-Nammu, the mighty warrior, king of Ur, king of Sumer and Akkad, establish equity in the land, banish abuse, violence, and strife. The orphan was not delivered up to the rich man; the widow was not delivered up to the powerful man." Many of its decrees revolve around the principle of compensation; payments in silver took the place of physical punishments. Thus a man who cut off another's foot was obliged to pay 10 silver

142

shekels. The fine for cutting off a nose, two-thirds of a mina, or 40 shekels, was more substantial.

The large sums of money levied as fines for various infractions may reflect the prosperity of Ur-Nammu's kingdom. His dynasty also appears better organized than its predecessor, the Akkadian empire, and not only in legal matters. A highly centralized bureaucratic hierarchy accounted to the king for everything in his realm, from a laborer's daily pay rate to the strength of the beer produced by state-controlled breweries.

Ur-Nammu himself did not live to see the full development of the system he had begun. According to a damaged, six-column tablet—the only known account of his fate—he died in combat after an 18-year reign, "abandoned on the battlefield like a crushed vessel." The tablet concludes with a lament against the gods for destroying a king who had served them well, but no details of his last campaign have been preserved.

Ur-Nammu's son, Shulgi, seems to have spent the first half of his long, 48-year reign at peace, but knowledge of his times remains spotty. Some scholars, for example, believe the law code attributed to Ur-Nammu was actually formulated by Shulgi. The historical facts pose more questions than they answer. Thus, for instance, the 19th year of Shulgi's reign is marked "Year the citizens of Ur were organized as spearmen"; his 26th was the "Year Simurum was destroyed"; his 27th the "Year Simurum was destroyed a second time"; and his 45th the "Year Simurum and Lulubum were destroyed a ninth time."

Did the "citizens of Ur" provide the king with a standing army or an ad-hoc force to deal with a sudden crisis? Was the unfortunate realm of Simurum rebuilt eight times in less than 20 years? The date lists provide no clue.

On the other hand, archaeologists have assembled a huge quantity of day-to-day administrative records, perhaps too many: Modern scholars have already published almost 30,000 examples, enough to swamp analysts for decades to come, and thousands more remain to be deciphered. These mundane reports paint a picture of a highly centralized, almost totalitarian state. At its apex stood the king, who, like Naram-Sin before him, claimed the status of a god.

Gold, agate, green bloodstone, and etched carnelian beads display the craftsmanship of Akkadian and Third Dynasty of Ur jewelers. When Ur fell, many of its artisans were taken as slaves by the Elamites, and thus their skills and technology were spread throughout the Near East.

Beginning with Shulgi, the king directly controlled substantial wealth, including workshops, textile mills, and the serfs and slaves who operated them. He put his own people in charge of the temples—much as Sargon had done with his daughter at Ur—to appropriate the immense temple revenues. In all sectors, the royal government dominated the empire's productive economy.

In the Sumerian heartland, each city-state was administered by a provincial governor who shared power with the district's military commander, a senior officer—likely to be a royal relative—who reported directly to the king. The bedrock of the state, however, remained the bureaucracy.

One of the most important institutions to officialdom was the *edubba*, the scribal school through which most of the state's administrators—not only the scribes—had to pass. King Shulgi himself had done so. According to one Sumerian riddle, "He whose eyes are not open enters it; he whose eyes are wide open comes out of it"—a reference not only to the advantages of education over ignorance but to the initiation its graduates received into the secrets of statecraft. In the edubba, all learned Sumerian, by this time in decline but still the language of record for business and government.

The tightly organized empire of Ur seemed rock solid and unchallengeable, as eternal as the Euphrates. But natural changes in the topography of the land, along with other, external factors, conspired to hasten the downfall of Sumer. The Euphrates itself, giver of life to the parched land, shifted its course, leaving some Sumerian riverside cities high and dry. And beyond Sumer's frontiers, the peoples of the desert and the mountains began to press in against the state as the power of Shulgi's heirs ebbed with alarming speed. In its usual laconic style, the King List counts down the names: "Amar-Sin, the son of Shulgi, reigned 9 years; Shu-Sin, the brother of Amar-Sin, reigned 9 years; Ibbi-Sin, the son of Shu-Sin, reigned 24 years." And there the counting—and the dynasty—stops.

Amar-Sin ruled much as his father had, but in Shu-Sin's time, the first reports of dangerous incursions begin to appear. They concerned the Martu, the Sumerian name for the Amorites of Syria and Arabia. They were regarded as unsettled and uncivilized, noted since Early Dynastic times as a people "who know no grain, who know no house nor town." Shu-Sin's fourth year was "Year when the wall of Martu was built." This fortification, built somewhere north of Ur, apparently was intended to stem the advancing tide.

A vaulted staircase leads out of the mausoleum of Shulgi, son of Ur-Nammu and one of the last great kings of Ur. During his long reign, Shulgi, by his own account a graduate of the Sumerian edubba, or school, lavishly supported the arts. Poets and composers repaid him in kind, writing long and laudatory hymns about his accomplishments.

By the end of Shu-Sin's reign, however, the Elamites to the east had added a new pressure, and under the strain of all-round attack, the realm began to show clear signs of internal failure, too. The post of provincial governor, a royal appointment in the reign of Shulgi, had increasingly become the hereditary prerogative of local aristocrats. Coupled with the vulnerability of communications to disruptive raids, schism and secession became the order of the day. Ibbi-Sin, Shu-Sin's son, would preside over a shrinking, impoverished state.

Letters between Ibbi-Sin and his increasingly insolent governors have survived to document the end of an empire. Food shortages became endemic in the capital, with prices rising 60-fold by the seventh year of Ibbi-Sin's reign. In desperation, the king ordered one Ishbi-Irra, governor of Isin, near Nippur, to buy up grain for him. The governor bought the grain but had problems with shipment. "The Martu—all of them—have entered the midst of the land and have seized the great fortresses one after the other. They are too strong for me, I am immobilized." Meanwhile, the governor added, the Martu also threatened Isin and Nippur itself: Would the king grant Ishbi-Irra the authority to defend both places? The king had no choice, but within a few years, Ishbi-Irra had claimed Isin as king in his own right.

Another governor reported that Ishbi-Irra, the usurper, controlled most of the Tigris and the Euphrates valleys and had killed or imprisoned Ibbi-Sin's few loyal supporters. The same official, though, declined to attack Ishbi-Irra with troops the king had provided, suggesting that the governor's own allegiance was somewhat shaky. Ibbi-Sin, trapped in hungry Ur, vented his spleen in a reply to his political appointee: Ishbi-Irra was "a worthless man, who is not of Sumerian seed." As for the Martu and the Elamites, the gods

would see that they neutralized each other and the hated Ishbi-Irra, too: "Now Enlil has stirred up the Martu from out of their land, they will strike down the Elamites and capture Ishbi-Irra. With the restoration of the land to its former place, its might will become known throughout all the lands."

No such restoration ever took place. Instead, the Elamites, presumably taking advantage of internal weaknesses, closed in around Ur. In 2004 BC they took the ancient city by storm, and Ibbi-Sin, whose grandfather had confidently ruled the land between the rivers, was carried to Elam to end his life in captivity.

Soon after Ur's destruction, a Sumerian poet wrote a great lament for the catastrophe, part of which is addressed to Ningal, consort of Nanna, the patron deity of the city: "O righteous woman whose city has been destroyed, how can you now exist! Your city has been made into ruins—you are no longer its mistress. Your people who have been led to the slaughter—you are no longer their queen. Your tears have become strange tears, your land weeps not. Your land like one who has multiplied shuts tight its mouth. Your city has been made into ruins; how can you exist! Your house has been laid bare; how has your heart led you on! Ur, the shrine, has been given over to the wind."

All was not quite lost. Ur was never of great political importance again—though the "worthless" Ishbi-Irra attempted to rebuild it soon after its destruction—but neither the city nor the culture that produced it would be truly lost. Indeed, the influx of Amorites into Sumer proved a crucial development in the long run. As they became civilized under the influence of that culture, they, in turn, helped transform it into something new—the great civilization of Babylonia.

The passage from Sumerian to Babylonian civilization represents a continuum in Mesopotamian history. Sumer's literary traditions would stretch on for centuries through the schoolrooms of Babylonia and Assyria. But the Sumerian roots of later Mesopotamian civilization were buried so deeply that in time they virtually disappeared beneath the great flowering that later sprouted above them, and in the end, Sumer was forgotten.

Almost 4,000 years later, the pick and trowel of archaeology and the furrowed brow of cuneiform scholarship would bring Sumer's ancient glories back into the light. It would be possible once again to write, as Ur's lamenting poet had written: "City, your name yet is, while you are ravaged."

SERVANTS TO THE GODS

In the beginning, there was water. The ancient sages of Sumer envisioned a primeval sea, present from the start of time, that spawned the universe of heaven and earth and its myriad inhabitants, all managed by a collection of divinities according to their personal plans and laws. Male and female, these gods existed in humanlike form—although they were invisible to the eyes of mortals—and required food and shelter in much the same way as people, whom the deities had created in their own image for the sole purpose of serving these basic needs.

In myths, hymns, proverbs, and lists passed down through oral tradition and eventually transcribed on stone and clay, the prolific Sumerians documented such beliefs, which governed their every thought and deed. Numbers of these written texts survived the onslaught of time in temple and palace libraries to tell of elaborate religious rituals, members of the pantheon, and a grim underworld. In addition, a pictorial record of Mesopo-

tamian belief exists in the many cylinder seals discovered among the ruins. Rolled out on clay, the relief impressions depict the gods with their sacred symbols as well as humble humans bearing offerings to the temples. And to suggest the awe the gods inspired, there are statues of worshipers such as the one above, eyes agog in the presence of a divinity.

The temples themselves—the hub of religious life in Sumer—provide another rich source of information and conjecture for the practices and beliefs described on the following pages. Frequently occupying premium sites in the cities, the sacred structures often displayed grand proportions and embellishments, which, together with their sheer numbers, reveal the prominence of religion in Mesopotamia. As civilization matured along the Tigris and the Euphrates, its temples grew higher and richer, monuments not only to the gods but also to the increasing complexity of the cultural revolution that the Sumerians had given birth to.

A POPULOUS PANTHEON

In the first days, in the very first days, when heaven had moved away from earth and earth had separated from heaven, the father set sail, Enki, the god of wisdom set sail.

FROM A SUMERIAN EPIC

The gods and goddesses of Sumer could have filled a city, so numerous were they. And for good reason: Everything from music, sex, and disease to the harvest and even such intangibles as wisdom worked by divine forces that were owned, and even bargained over, by the immortals. In addition, each town had a patron god, and individuals maintained their personal divinities.

Three creator gods—An of the heavens, Enlil of the atmosphere, and Enki of the waters—stood at the top of the hierarchy. But the Sumerians also placed great importance on Inanna, later known as Ishtar, who controlled such disparate components of life as sexual love, fertility, and war. Ninhursag, known as the "mother of the gods," enjoyed the greatest status of the mother goddesses, one of whom, Bau, may be represented by the statue pictured at right, identified by the goose—apparently her symbol—at her side.

Humanity held the gods, like themselves, to be essentially moral. But from the loftiest member to the lowliest, they were all subject to human foibles, suffering the passions of love, hatred, and jealousy, bickering among themselves, getting drunk, and even committing an occasional evil deed.

Some 5,000 years ago, this life-size lime-stone face from Uruk may have graced a statue of a goddess, possibly Inanna. Her brows join—a sign of beauty—and were once inlaid, like the eyes themselves, with such exotic imports as shell and lazuli.

A powerful trio of immortals appears in this impression from a cylinder seal dating to around 2200 BC. Winged Inanna—here symbolizing the planet Venus, or morning star—hovers over Utu, who rises from the mountains like the sun he represents, while fish-filled waters flow from Enki, standing by his mythic two-faced vizier, Usmu (far right).

This four-inch-high terra-cotta head—a sculpture from the town of Girsu that dates to the late third millennium BC— is known to represent a divinity, albeit an anonymous one, by his special tiered crown composed of horns.

A FEARFUL DEPENDENCE ON THE DEITIES

Worship your god every day. Have a freewill offering for your god, for this is proper toward a god. Prayer, supplication, and prostration offer him daily, then your prayer will be granted.

AKKADIAN TEXT

In an unpredictable world where natural disaster could blight the cradle of civilization at any moment, humankind lived in dread of the gods. Like most ancient peoples, Sumerians attributed blessing and calamity to divine will—though they apparently never felt their own behavior brought about misfortunes, for none of their prayers or hymns express the notion of guilt or sin that would crop up in later societies.

Preoccupied with the pantheon's terrible power, the Sumerians looked to the gods for mercy and protection and devoted vast resources to meeting the needs of the divine with food and drink, lodging, and works of art. The alabaster statue at right, dedicated by an official named Ebihil and found at the Temple of Ishtar at Mari, represents Ebihil in perpetual worship. Such votive figures enabled an anxious citizenry to tend to daily life without neglecting the divinities.

Despite the unpredictable hardships of an earthly existence, though, prospects in the afterlife loomed worse still. In the dark, dusty Lower World, or Land of No Return, even the most privileged during life roamed eternally naked and thirsty after death.

Clasping their hands reverently and gazing heaven-
ward, these statues—most of them from the Square
Temple at Eshnunna—served as stone proxies for the
individual citizens who placed them there.

Dedicated around 2050 BC to the underworld god Ningizzida by "Nikala, the
shepherd of fat sheep," a white stone seal
formed this impression of a worshiper being led to a god.

Found at the temple of the
goddess Inanna at Nippur,
this intimate portrait of a
couple was carved from a single piece of gypsum, with in-
set eyes of lapis lazuli, shell,
and bitumen.

SACRED PRACTICES OF THE SUMERIAN CULTS

They prepare bread in date syrup for her. They pour wine and honey for her at sunrise. The gods and people of Sumer go to her with food and drink. They feed Inanna in the pure clean place.

FROM A HYMN TO INANNA

Amid the wafting scents of burning aromatics brought in from Mediterranean forests, the inhabitants of Sumer conducted a rich variety of rituals in the often magnificent temples that they built to serve as homes to the gods. Here, on the sacred floors and altars, animals regularly met their deaths through religious sacrifice, and each day the tables were laid with such fare as bread, fish, cakes, fruit, and wine to fortify the temple god and his or her family. Crafted in human form and treated as if they were living beings, cult statues of the divinities presided over these banquets and "accepted" the offerings, which afterward passed to the king for his consumption. Having been "blessed" during the serving ritual, the food was believed to confer divine blessings upon the king—and, by extension, upon his people.

In addition to being fed, the statues were showered with gifts of clothing and jewelry. A large temple staff adorned the figures in their finery, entertained them with music and circuslike acts—and even transported them to neighboring temples so that they might visit with other members of their divine fam-

ily. The staff could number more than 200 men and women, who held such diverse roles as snake charmer, barber, weaver, scribe, and priest of lamentation or purification. Although Sumerian texts do not specifically mention eunuchs, many of the temple singers apparently displayed telltale womanly traits, as indicated by the figure shown at far right, a male by the name of Ur-Nanshe.

Probably an en, or priest-king, the net-skirted figure in this seal impression dating to 3100 BC carries offerings to the Temple of Inanna, followed by an assistant bearing further gifts.

ROYAL OBLIGATIONS TO THE DIVINE POWERS

In a dream, the god Ningirsu came up to Gudea and said: "You will build the house for me; let me give you the sign, let me tell of my rites in accordance with the holy stars."

FROM GUDEA'S CYLINDER STONE

Among the most important of the Sumerian kings' responsibilities was the building and maintenance of the temples. Only by tending religiously to these could a ruler—regarded by his people as the living link between humans and the gods—be expected to invite and encourage the blessings that the divinities could confer.

Artifacts uncovered throughout the ruins of Sumer document this obligation, including figures of rulers in symbolic construction roles *(right)*. One of the most significant finds, however, is a pair of large stone cylinders that contain the text of a masterpiece of ancient literature: a poem describing Gudea's inspiration for renovating Eninnu, the temple of the god Ningirsu.

Figurines—often fashioned in the likeness of the ruler or a deity, like the kneeling copper god pictured at right who holds a building peg—were buried in the foundations of new temples during construction rituals in order to purify the sacred area. In erecting their splendid temples, rulers took great pride: "Fashion artfully gold and silver on my behalf," implores an ancient hymn. "Let them cut the pure lapis lazuli from the lumps. In Uruk a holy 'mountain' let them lavishly decorate."

In a detail from a seal impression, two men help build a temple tower. To the right of the man in the tasseled skirt stands another figure holding aloft bricks with the plano-convex shape typical of the Sumerian culture.

A basketful of mud used for mortar perches symbolically on the head of a bronze image of King Ur-Nammu, builder of the great Ur ziggurat. This foundation figure came from the Temple of Enlil at Nippur.

Known by the inscription in the polished diorite to represent Gudea, Lagash governor around 2120 BC, this headless statue holds a primitive blueprint of a temple—shown above in detail—in its lap. The plan, believed by Gudea to have been dictated by the god Ningirsu, came to the ruler in a dream.

In your house on high, in your beloved house, I will come to live, up above in your cedar-perfumed mountain, in your citadel, O Nanna, in your mansion of Ur I will come to live.

FROM A SONG

Throughout history humans have linked high places with the divine: Ancient Egyptians crafted giant pyramids for their god-kings, Moses brought the Ten Commandments down from Mount Sinai, and across the North American continent and in Central America, Indians built temples upon great mounds of earth and stone. Constructing their temples on platforms, the people of Sumer also situated the homes of their gods a little closer to heaven, over time erecting higher and higher monuments, in most cases simply atop the old ones. The steplike tower known as a ziggurat—the culmination of the platform temple—itself appears to emulate a mountain, and indeed, many of the ziggurats

prominent in the important cities of Sumer featured the word *mountain* in their names.

Most renowned among the ziggurat builders, Ur-Nammu of the Third Dynasty of Ur ordered the construction of the great ziggurat in his city to honor the moon god Nanna. Shown at right in a modern photograph with an overlay reflecting its original appearance some 4,000 years ago, the mud-brick monument—the best preserved of any that remain in Mesopotamia— once soared 80 feet high and measured 150 by 200 feet at its base, according to the calculations of Leonard Woolley, who excavated the temple mound with exquisite care during the 1920s and 1930s. A magnificent triple staircase led to the first of its three levels, and like other Sumerian temples, the ziggurat probably supported a shrine at its peak, where the Sacred Marriage ritual between the king and a priestess is thought to have taken place. A feat of sophisticated engineering, the massive walls bowed both horizontally and vertically in order to create the illusion from a distance that they were straight.

God of the moon and the patron deity of Ur, Nanna sits before a worshipful Ur-Nammu in a fragment of the Stele of Ur-Nammu, found in the city of the great ziggurat. Offering libations to Nanna, the king pours out what may be wine, water, oil, or the blood of a newly sacrificed animal.

THE PIONEERS OF CIVILIZATION

It was in the ancient Near East, sometime around 8000 BC, that humankind took its first tentative steps beyond the primeval existence of the hunter-gatherer. The domestication of plants and animals permitted the forebears of the ancient Sumerians to settle more or less permanently in one place.

But the transition from roving to sedentary lifestyle was hardly abrupt. At Jarmo, a settlement in northeastern Iraq, archaeologists probing a layer dating to about 7000 BC found evidence of wild foods alongside the bones of domesticated animals and cultivated grain. Clearly, the people continued to rely on an opportunistic diet while they experimented with rudimentary agriculture and animal husbandry.

Several cultures flourished in northern Mesopotamia during the seventh and sixth millennia. Relics from the lower levels of Tell Hassuna include stone and bone tools, husking trays, flat stones for grinding flour, and crude baked-clay vessels. Upper layers contained a much finer pottery, called—like the culture it represents—Samarran. At numerous sites throughout the region another type of pottery, the brilliantly painted Halaf ware, dating to about 5700 BC, has turned up, indicating trade between the widely scattered settlements of this period. Around this time, too, the practice of irrigation, first developed on a significant scale by the Samarrans, came into being. These early cultures had now mastered the two technologies—domestication and irrigation—necessary for settling the regions of southern Mesopotamia.

UBAID PERIOD
5900-4000 BC

STYLIZED FIGURINE

Concurrent with the sixth-millennium cultures in the north, farming communities grew up on the alluvial plain of the Tigris and the Euphrates rivers. The boundless waters of the Tigris and the Euphrates were tapped by means of an extensive infrastructure of canals to irrigate the parched, but potentially fertile, soil.

With human intervention, the land between the rivers blossomed spectacularly. Evidence at sites such as Tell al-Ubaid—for which this period is named—revealed that, for the first time, a farmer could produce more than his family needed and sell or barter the surplus to his fellow citizens, who, in turn, could devote their energies to other pursuits. The concept of professions was thus born. Furthermore, the agricultural surfeit meant that people could gather together in ever larger numbers; villages became towns, and society became more stratified as a result.

Theology evidently played an important role in daily life, with temples serving as the focal point of the towns; the Ubaid period settlement of Eridu contains the ruins of 12 temples superimposed on the same site. All the prerequisites were now in place for the successors of the Ubaid period to become full-fledged urbanites.

URUK PERIOD
4000-3000 BC

ALABASTER VASE

While most of the world still sheltered in caves and crude huts and foraged for a living, the citizens of Uruk in southern Mesopotamia had, by around 3500 BC, built a city of thousands out of little more than sun-dried mud bricks. Theirs was a society of distinct classes—including professional bureaucrats and theocrats—ruled by a political and religious elite.

The government of Uruk supported itself by imposing taxes on the citizenry and conscripting labor for public-works projects. In return, ordinary men and women received spiritual succor in the temples and access to exotic foreign merchandise and mass-produced consumer goods, such as pottery.

Uruk's artists also created singular works of unsurpassed beauty and realism for the city's elite and for its gods. Meanwhile, commerce and trade grew rapidly in the bustling city and led to what is undoubtedly Sumer's greatest legacy to humankind—writing. The people of Uruk devised a system to record their business transactions by engraving simple pictographs into clay tablets. The oldest examples, from around 3300 BC, list specific quantities of basic commodities such as grain, beer, and livestock.

EARLY DYNASTIC PERIOD
3000-2350 BC

STATUE FROM ROYAL TOMBS AT UR

AKKADIAN PERIOD
2350-2150 BC

BRONZE HEAD OF AKKADIAN RULER

NEO-SUMERIAN PERIOD
2150-2000 BC

STATUE OF GUDEA

Other cities emerged on the plains of Sumer in Uruk's wake. Encompassing small, outlying settlements as well as the adjacent fields and irrigation systems, these population centers developed into politically independent city-states. All Sumerians worshiped the same pantheon of gods, but each city-state had its own patron deity and ruling dynasty.

Perhaps inevitably, conflicts arose among these city-states over relative wealth and the distribution of vital natural resources, mainly water. The world's first armies crisscrossed the dusty plains as the monarchs of Kish, Lagash, Umma, Ur, and the other city-states vied for supremacy in a seemingly endless series of internecine wars. The net result was a depletion of manpower and capital and an erosion of rights for the common people. To finance their military ventures, rulers raised taxes, arbitrarily seized property, and assessed fees for almost every activity imaginable.

Around 2400 BC an enlightened despot named Urukagina ascended the throne of Lagash, avowing that a ruler's responsibility extended to rich and poor alike. He was, however, overthrown less than a decade later by Lugalzaggesi, king of Lagash's old enemy Umma.

The warring city-states of Sumer were forcibly unified under one ruler, Sargon the Great, who, ironically, was not even Sumerian. Under Sargon—and, later, his grandson Naram-Sin—the Akkadians, a Semitic people who had settled in the northern part of the alluvial plain possibly during the fourth millennium, ruled Sumer and dispatched their conquering armies beyond the boundaries of Mesopotamia.

Eventually, though, the world's first empire crumbled under the twin threats of internal rebellion from the subjugated city-states and external pressure from less-settled tribes, such as the Gutians, on the periphery. The capital city of Agade was destroyed—its location remains unknown—and Akkadian rule in Sumer came to an end.

Much information relating to the Akkadian period comes from written records, for, by this time, the original pictographs used by Uruk's citizens had evolved into an "alphabet" of abstract symbols—called cuneiform script—that could express the full range of human thought. Although their spoken languages were quite dissimilar, both Sumerians and Akkadians used cuneiform to create epic literature, lyric poetry, and even propaganda.

After the collapse of Sargon's dynasty, Sumer enjoyed a brief revival of political power. The city-state of Lagash, which had chafed under Akkadian domination, regained some of its lost autonomy. Around 2140 its ruler, Gudea, set about rebuilding temples as a symbolic act of independence. Twenty years later, venerable Uruk, under King Utuhegal, drove the Gutians out of Sumer altogether.

In 2112 Ur-Nammu, whom Utuhegal had appointed governor of Ur, ascended the throne, thus founding the Third Dynasty of Ur. Many of his works survive, including the great ziggurat, built around 2100, and the oldest legal code ever found. Ur-Nammu's kingdom was even more tightly organized than Sargon's, with a highly centralized bureaucracy accountable to the king for everything and everyone in his realm.

Ur-Nammu ruled for 18 years; his son Shulgi for 48 more. After that, however, the reigns become more abbreviated, and Ur's authority inexorably declined. By about 2000 BC Sumer as a political entity had disappeared. Even so, its glory was preserved in the literary traditions of its successors, the great civilizations of Babylonia and Assyria.

ACKNOWLEDGMENTS

The editors wish to thank the following individuals and institutions for their valuable assistance in the preparation of this volume: Fayadh Taha Al Fayadh, Rome; Brigitte Baumbusch, Florence; Rainer Michael Boehmer, Deutsches Archäologisches Institut, Berlin; Jenny Vorys Canby, University Museum, University of Pennsylvania, Philadelphia; Herma Chang, British Museum, London; Irmgard Ernstmeier, Hirmer Verlag, Munich; Irving Finkel, British Museum, London; Ann C. Gunter, Arthur M. Sackler Gallery, Washington, D.C.; Douglas M. Haller, University Museum, University of Pennsylvania, Philadelphia; Donald Hansen, New York University, New York; Jean-Louis Huot, Paris; Iraqi National Museum, Baghdad; Diana Kirkbride-Helbaek, Aarhus, Denmark; Heidi Klein, Bildarchiv Preussischer Kulturbesitz, Berlin; Evelyn Klengel, Vorderasiatisches Museum, Staatliche Museen, Berlin; Karin Maul, Staatliche Kunstsammlungen, Dresden; Ministry of Information, Baghdad; Ursula Moortgat-Correns, Vorderasiatisches Institut, Freie Universität, Berlin; Maurizio Necci, Rome; Joan Oates, Cambridge University, Cambridge; Alessandro Pezzati, University Museum, University of Pennsylvania, Philadelphia; Adnan Rasem, Rome; Julian Read, British Museum, London.

PICTURE CREDITS

The sources for the illustrations in this volume are listed below. Credits from left to right are separated by semicolons, from top to bottom by dashes.

Cover: © The Detroit Institute of Arts, Founders Society Purchase, Robert H. Tannahill Foundation Fund. Background Robert Harding Picture Library, London. End paper: Art by Paul Breeden. 6, 7: © Jonathan T. Wright/Bruce Coleman, Inc. 8: Réunion des Musées Nationaux (R.M.N.), Paris. 11: Bibliothèque Nationale, Paris. 14, 15: The University Museum, University of Pennsylvania (neg. no. T4-423); Kunsthistorisches Museum, Vienna/Bildarchiv Preussischer Kulturbesitz, Berlin. 16: U.S. Geological Survey/EROS Data Center—Juris Zarins; Jean-Loup Charmet, Paris. 18: Copyright British Museum, London. 19: Erwin Böhm, Mainz, Germany. 20: R.M.N., Paris. 21: Louvre, Paris/Bildarchiv Preussischer Kulturbesitz, Berlin. 22-24: Copyright British Museum, London. 25: Archives Photographiques, Paris/S.P.A.D.E.M. 26, 27: Courtesy Editions Les Belles Lettres, from *Histoire du Costume dans L'Antiquité Classique, L'ORIENT, Égypte, Mésopotamie, Syrie, Phénicie,* by Léon Heuzey and Jacques Heuzey, DR. 28, 29: Copyright British Museum, London. 30, 31: The University Museum, University of Pennsylvania (neg. no. G8-5303); (neg. no. G8-5811). 33: University of Newcastle upon Tyne, England. 35: Prof. Karlheinz Kessler, Emskirchen, Germany. 36, 37: Hirmer Fotoarchiv, Munich. 38, 39: Tilmann Eickhoff, Ehingen/Donau, Germany. 40, 41: David Lees, Florence. 42, 43: Georg Gerster, Zurich. 44: Scala, Florence/Iraq Museum, Baghdad. 46: Iraq Museum, Baghdad, from *Atlas of Mesopotamia,* by Martin A. Beek, published by Thomas Nelson & Sons Ltd, 1962. 47: Foto Claus Hansmann, Munich/Iraq Museum, Baghdad. 48: Hubert Josse, Paris. 49: Copyright British Museum, London. 50, 51: Robert Harding Picture Library, London—copyright British Museum, London. 52: Antonio Invernizzi, Turin, Italy/Iraq Museum, Baghdad. 53: R.M.N., Paris. 54, 55: J. Oates, Cambridge, England—Robert J. Braidwood, courtesy The Oriental Institute of The University of Chicago; Picturepoint Ltd., London; Hirmer Fotoarchiv, Munich/Iraq Museum, Baghdad (2); copyright British Museum, London; Staatliche Museen zu Berlin/Preussischer Kulturbesitz Vorderasiatisches Museum, photo by Reinhard Saczewski, 1992; copyright British Museum, London; Hirmer Fotoarchiv, Munich/Iraq Museum, Baghdad. Base art by Time-Life Books. 56: Foto Claus Hansmann, Munich/Aleppo National Museum, Syria. 57: Art by Time-Life Books. 58: Photo Jean Mazenod, *L'Art Antique du Proche-Orient,* éditions Citadelles & Mazenod, Paris. 59: From M. E. L. Mallowan and J. Cruikshank Rose, *Excavations at Tell Arpachiyah Iraq,* Vol. II, Part I. London: British School of Archaeology in Iraq, 1933, Plate II, photographed by 30th Squadron R.A.F., courtesy Library of Congress, neg. no. 303129. 60, 61: Foto Claus Hansmann, Munich/Iraq Museum, Baghdad. 62, 63: Background Robert Harding Picture Library, London. Giraudon, Paris; art by Time-Life Books—Robert Colton, courtesy Smithsonian Institution, Washington, D.C. (3); Staatliche Museen zu Berlin/Preussischer Kulturbesitz Vorderasiatisches Museum. 64: Hirmer Fotoarchiv, Munich/Iraq Museum, Baghdad. 66, 67: J. Oates, Cambridge, England. 68, 69: J. L. Huot, Paris. 70, 71: Courtesy The Oriental Institute of The University of Chicago (2); Tony Howarth/Woodfin Camp, Inc. 72, 73: Dr. Diana Kirkbride, from *Fifty Years of Mesopotamian Discovery,* British School of Archaeology in Iraq (London)—Foto Claus Hansmann, Munich/National Museum, Damascus (2). 75: Copyright British Museum, London. 76: Staatliche Museen zu Berlin/Preussischer Kulturbesitz, Vorderasiatisches Museum, photograph by Jürgen Liepe, 1991; R.M.N., Paris—Staatliche Museen zu Berlin/Preussischer Kulturbesitz, Vorderasiatisches Muse-

BIBLIOGRAPHY

BOOKS

Amiet, Pierre. *Art of the Ancient Near East.* Translated by John Shepley and Claude Choquet. New York: Harry N. Abrams, 1977.

Bacon, Edward (Ed.). *The Great Archaeologists.* Indianapolis: Bobbs-Merrill, 1976.

Baumann, Hans. *The Land of Ur.* Translated by Stella Humphries. London: Oxford University Press, 1969.

Beek, Martin A. *Atlas of Mesopotamia.* Edited by H. H. Rowley, translated by D. R. Welsh. New York: Thomas Nelson and Sons, 1962.

Bermant, Chaim, and Michael Weitzman. *Ebla: A Revelation in Archaeology.* New York: Quadrangle/New York Times Book Co., 1979.

Black, Jeremy, and Anthony Green. *Gods, Demons and Symbols of Ancient Mesopotamia: An Illustrated Dictionary.* Austin: University of Texas Press, 1992.

Braidwood, Linda. *Digging beyond the Tigris.* New York: Henry Schuman, 1953.

Campbell, Joseph. *Historical Atlas of World Mythology,* Vol. 2: *The Way of the Seeded Earth.* New York: Harper & Row, 1988.

Caubet, Annie, and Marthe Bernus-Taylor. *The Louvre: Near Eastern Antiquities.* Translated by Alexandra Trone. London: Scala Publications, 1991.

Christie, Agatha. *An Autobiography.* New York: Dodd, Mead, 1977.

Collon, Dominique:
First Impressions: Cylinder Seals in the Ancient Near East. Chicago: University of Chicago Press, 1987.
Near Eastern Seals. London: British Museum Publications, 1990.

Crawford, Harriet. *Sumer and the Sumerians.* Cambridge: Cambridge University Press, 1991.

Cultural Atlas of Mesopotamia and the Ancient Near East. Oxford: Equinox, 1990.

Curtis, John (Ed.). *Fifty Years of Mesopotamian Discovery.* London: British School of Archaeology in Iraq, 1982.

Fagan, Brian M. *Return to Babylon.* Boston: Little, Brown, 1979.

Finegan, Jack. *Archaeological History of the Ancient Middle East.* New York: Dorset Press, 1979.

Forbes, R. J. *Studies in Ancient Technology.* Leiden, The Netherlands: E. J. Brill, 1955.

Frankfort, Henri. *The Art and Architecture of the Ancient Orient.* London: Penguin Books, 1970.

Frankfort, Henri, H. A. Frankfort, John A. Wilson, Thorkild Jacobsen, and William A. Irwin. *The Intellectual Adventure of Ancient Man.* Chicago: University of Chicago Press, 1946.

Gabriel, Richard A., and Karen S. Metz. *From Sumer to Rome.* New York: Greenwood Press, 1991.

Glubok, Shirley (Ed.). *Discovering the Royal Tombs at Ur.* London: Collier-Macmillan, 1969.

Gowlett, John. *Ascent to Civilization.* London: Collins, 1984.

Groenewegen-Frankfort, H. A., and Bernard Ashmole. *Art of the Ancient World.* Edited by H. W. Janson. Englewood Cliffs, N.J.: Prentice-Hall, 1971.

Hallo, William W., and William Kelly Simpson. *The Ancient Near East: A History.* New York: Harcourt Brace Jovanovich, 1971.

Hamblin, Dora Jane, and the Editors of Time-Life Books. *The First Cities* (Emergence of Man series). New York: Time-Life Books, 1973.

Henrickson, Elizabeth F., and Ingolf Thuesen (Eds.). *Upon this Foundation.* Copenhagen: Museum Tusculanum Press, 1989.

Heuzey, Léon, and Jacques Heuzey. *Histoire du Costume dans L'Antiquité Classique L'Orient.* Paris: Editions Les Belles Lettres, 1935.

Hodges, Henry. *Technology in the Ancient World.* New York: Alfred A. Knopf, 1970.

The Horizon Book of Lost Worlds. New York: American Heritage, 1962.

Hrouda, Barthel. *Der Alte Orient.* Munich: C. Bertelsmann, 1991.

Jacobsen, Thorkild. *The Treasures of Darkness: A History of Mesopotamian Religion.* New Haven: Yale University Press, 1976.

Jakob-Rost, Lian, Evelyn Klengel-Brandt, Joachim Marzahn, and Ralf-B. Wartke. *Das Vorderasiatische Museum.* Mainz: Verlag Philipp von Zabern, 1992.

Johansen, Flemming. *Mesopotamia:*

Copenhagen Studies in Assyriology, Vol. 6: *Statues of Gudea, Ancient and Modern.* Copenhagen: Akademisk Forlag, 1978.

Kramer, Samuel Noah:
History Begins at Sumer. Philadelphia: University of Pennsylvania Press, 1981.
The Sacred Marriage Rite: Aspects of Faith, Myth, and Ritual in Ancient Sumer. Bloomington: Indiana University Press, 1969.
The Sumerians: Their History, Culture, and Character. Chicago: University of Chicago Press, 1963.

Kramer, Samuel Noah, and the Editors of Time-Life Books. *Cradle of Civilization* (Great Ages of Man series). Alexandria: Time-Life Books, 1978.

The Land between Two Rivers. Edited by Ezio Quarantelli, translated by Juliet Haydock and Michael Binns. Turin, Italy: Il Quadrante Edizioni, 1985.

Langdon, S. *Excavations at Kish.* Paris: Librairie Orientaliste, 1924.

Leonard, Jonathan Norton, and the Editors of Time-Life Books. *The First Farmers* (Emergence of Man series). New York: Time-Life Books, 1973.

Lloyd, Seton:
The Archaeology of Mesopotamia. London: Thames and Hudson, 1984 (rev. ed.).
Foundations in the Dust: The Story of Mesopotamian Exploration. London: Thames and Hudson, 1980 (rev. ed.).
Sumer: A Journal of Archaeology in Iraq. Baghdad: Directorate-General of Antiquities, 1947.

Lloyd, Seton, and Hans Wolfgang Müller. *Ancient Architecture.* New York: Electa/Rizzoli, 1980.

McCall, Henrietta. *Mesopotamian Myths.* London: British Museum Publications, 1990.

McIntosh, Jane. *The Practical Archaeologist: How We Know What We Know about the Past.* New York: Facts On File Publications, 1986.

Mallowan, Agatha Christie. *Come, Tell Me How You Live.* New York: Dodd, Mead, 1974.

Mallowan, M. E. L.:
Early Mesopotamia and Iran. New York: McGraw-Hill, 1965.

Mallowan's Memoirs. New York: Dodd, Mead, 1977.

Matthiae, Paolo. *Ebla: An Empire Rediscovered.* Garden City, N.Y.: Doubleday, 1981.

Millard, Alan. *Treasures from Bible Times.* Tring, Herts, England: Lion Publishing, 1985.

Moorey, P. R. S. *The Ancient Near East.* Oxford: Ashmolean Museum, 1987.

Moortgat, Anton. *The Art of Ancient Mesopotamia: The Classical Art of the Near East.* London: Phaidon Publishers, 1969.

Nissen, Hans J. *The Early History of the Ancient Near East, 9000-2000 B.C.* Chicago: University of Chicago Press, 1988.

Oates, David, and Joan Oates. *The Rise of Civilization.* New York: E. P. Dutton, 1976.

Oates, Joan. *Babylon.* London: Thames and Hudson, 1986 (rev. ed.).

Oppenheim, A. Leo. *Ancient Mesopotamia: Portrait of a Dead Civilization.* Chicago: University of Chicago Press, 1977.

Parrot, André. *Sumer: The Dawn of Art.* Translated by Stuart Gilbert and James Emmons. New York: Golden Press, 1961.

Payne, Blanche. *History of Costume: From the Ancient Egyptians to the Twentieth Century.* New York: Harper & Row, 1965.

Pettinato, Giovanni. *The Archives of Ebla: An Empire Inscribed in Clay.* Garden City, N.Y.: Doubleday, 1981.

Postgate, J. N. *Early Mesopotamia: Society and Economy at the Dawn of History.* London: Routledge, 1992.

Pritchard, James B. (Ed.). *The Ancient Near East: Supplementary Texts and Pictures Relating to the Old Testament.* Princeton, N.J.: Princeton University Press, 1969.

Quest for the Past. Pleasantville, N.Y.: Reader's Digest Association, 1984.

Reade, Julian:
Assyrian Sculpture. Cambridge, Mass.: Harvard University Press, 1983.
Mesopotamia. London: British Museum Press, 1991.

Redman, Charles. *The Rise of Civilization.* San Francisco: W. H. Freeman, 1978.

Ringgren, Helmer. *Religions of the Ancient Near East.* Translated by John Sturdy. Philadelphia: Westminster Press, 1973.

Roaf, Michael. *Cultural Atlas of Mesopotamia and the Ancient Near East.* New York: Facts On File Publications, 1990.

Roux, Georges. *Ancient Iraq.* Harmondsworth, Middlesex: Penguin Books, 1980 (2nd ed.).

The Royal Game of Ur: A Game for 2 Players. London: British Museum, 1991.

Safar, Fuad, Mohammad Ali Mustafa, and Seton Lloyd. *Eridu.* Baghdad: State Organization of Antiquities and Heritage, 1981.

Sampson, Geoffrey. *Writing Systems: A Linguistic Introduction.* London: Hutchinson & Co., 1985.

Schmandt-Besserat, Denise. *Before Writing.* (Vols. 1 and 2). Austin: University of Texas Press, 1992.

Strommenger, Eva. *Fünf Jahrtausende Mesopotamien.* Munich: Hirmer Verlag, 1962.

Teissier, Beatrice. *Ancient Near Eastern Cylinder Seals from the Marcopoli Collection.* Berkeley: University of California Press, 1984.

Walker, C. B. F. *Cuneiform.* London: British Museum, 1989.

Wenke, Robert J. *Patterns in Prehistory.* New York: Oxford Press, 1990.

Winstone, H. V. F.:
Uncovering the Ancient World. New York: Facts On File Publications, 1985.
Woolley of Ur: The Life of Sir Leonard Woolley. London: Secker & Warburg, 1990.

Wolkstein, Diane, and Samuel Noah Kramer. *Inanna: Queen of Heaven and Earth.* New York: Harper & Row, 1983.

Woolley, C. Leonard:
The Sumerians. New York: W. W. Norton, 1965.
Ur 'of the Chaldees.' Ithaca, N.Y.: Cornell University Press, 1982 (rev. ed.).
World Atlas of Archaeology. New York: Portland House, 1985.

PERIODICALS

Adams, Robert M. "The Origin of Cities." *Scientific American,* Sept. 1960.

Asian Art. "Mesopotamian Art in the Louvre." Winter 1992.

Badler, Virginia R., Patrick E. McGovern, and Rudolph H. Michel. "Chemical Evidence for Ancient Beer." *Nature,* Nov. 5, 1992.

Braidwood, Robert J.:
"The Agricultural Revolution." *Scientific American,* Sept. 1960.
"Discovering the World's Earliest Village Community: The Claims of Jarmo as the Cradle of Civilisation." *Illustrated London News,* Dec. 15, 1951.

Butterfield, Herbert. "The Scientific Revolution." *Scientific American,* Sept. 1960.

"Deposits Inside Jar Appear to be 5000-Year-Old Beer." *Washington Post,* Nov. 6, 1992.

Expedition (University Museum, University of Pennsylvania), Fall 1977.

Hamblin, Dora Jane. "Has the Garden of Eden Been Located at Last?" *Smithsonian,* May 1977.

Hartman, Louis F., and A. P. Oppenheim. "On Beer and Brewing Techniques in Ancient Mesopotamia." *Journal of the American Oriental Society,* Dec. 10, 1950.

Huot, Jean-Louis. "Villes: Les Précurseurs." *Science et Vie,* March 1992.

Katz, Solomon, and Fritz Maytag. *Archaeology,* July/August 1991.

Katz, Solomon, and Mary M. Voigt. *Expedition,* Vol. 28, no. 2.

La Fay, Howard. "Ebla: Splendor of an Unknown Empire." *National Geographic,* Dec. 1978.

Legrain, L. "The Boudoir of Queen Shubad." *Museum Journal* (Museum of the University of Pennsylvania), Sept./Dec. 1929.

Saint-Blanquat, Henri de. "The Oldest House in the World." *Le Point,* May 14, 1990.

Severy, Merle. "Iraq: Crucible of Civilization." *National Geographic,* May 1991.

Steinmann, Marion. " 'Chicken Scratches' Written in Clay Yield Their Secrets." *Smithsonian,* Dec. 1988.

Turnbull, Priscilla. "Bones of Palegawra." *Natural History Magazine,* Sept. 1967.

Wilford, John Noble. "Jar in Iranian

Ruins Betrays Beer Drinkers of 3500 B.C." *New York Times,* Nov. 5, 1992.

Woolley, C. Leonard. "Ur of the Chaldees: More Royal Tombs." *Museum Journal* (Museum of the University of Pennsylvania), March 1929.

Zarins, Juris. "The Early Settlement of Southern Mesopotamia: A Review of Recent Historical, Geological, and Archaeological Research." *Journal of the American Oriental Society,* Jan./March 1992.

OTHER

"Ebla to Damascus: Art and Archaeology of Ancient Syria." Catalog. Washington, D.C.: Smithsonian Institution Traveling Exhibition Service, 1985.

"Préhistoire de la Mésopotamie." Report. Paris: Editions du Centre National de la Recherche Scientifique, 1987.

"The Royal City of Susa." Catalog. New York: Metropolitan Museum of Art, 1992.

"Sumer, Assur, Babylone." Catalog. Mainz: Philipp von Zabern, 1979.

INDEX

Christie, Agatha: 49, 58, 59, 60, 61, 86
Constantinople: 17, 29
Cooper, Frederick: views of ruins at Nimrud, *23*
Cranach, Lucas, the Elder: painting by, *14-15*
Crete: 123
Crimean War: archaeological activity interrupted by, 22
Cuneiform: 12, 13, 18-20, 76, 102, 115, 119, *123,* 159; development of scholarly dictionary for, *97;* efforts at decipherment, 22-24, 25-26, 120, 133, 134, 146; translated excerpts, 132-133
Curse of Agade: 125, 128
Cyrus the Great: 18

D

Dagan (deity): 123, 137
Daily Telegraph: 26
Damascus: 133
Darius (king): 18, 19
Delougaz, Pinhas: 96
Department of Oriental Antiquities (British Museum): 25
Dilmun: 123
Diyala River: 34, 96
Dumuzi (deity): 102
Dur Sharrukin: 21

E

Eannatum (king): 106-107
Early Dynastic period: 55, 96, 98, 109, 159
Ebihil: votive statue of, *150*
Ebla: 136-137, 142; excavation of royal palace at, *130-131,* 132; rediscovery of, 132; tablets recovered from royal archives of, 130, 132-133, *134*
Eblaite: 134
L'Ecole des Beaux-Arts: 27
Eden, Garden of: 12, 45, 74; in Sumerian myth and biblical story, *14-17*
Edubba: 144
Egypt: Mesopotamian influences, 57; trade with, 136
Ekur temple: 125, 128, 142
Elam: 123, 126, 145, 146
Elamite: inscriptions, 18, 22, 133
El Hibba: excavations at, 28
En: 152
Enheduanna: as high priestess of Ur, *122,* 123-124
Eninnu temple: 154
Enki (deity): 14, 46, 47, 148, 149

Enlil (deity): 102-103, 107, 108, 122, 123, 125, 146, 148
Enmebaragesi (king): 101
Enna-Dagan: 136
Ensis: 119, 139
Epic of Gilgamesh: See Gilgamesh epic
Erech: 53
Eridu: 57-58, 61, 68, 74; artifacts found at, *47;* cemetery at, 48; excavations at, 45, *46,* 47-49, 52; original Sumerian shrine, 46, 47, 98; temples at, 46, 53, 158; Ubaid influence in, 53; ziggurat at, 45, 46, 47, 48
Eshnunna: 151
Euphrates River: 12, 14, *map* 16, 27, 33, 35, 36, 39, 41, 42, 45, 57, 65, 75, 83, 84, 92, 120, 123, 136, 144, 145, 147, 158
Eve: 14, 15
Eye Temple (Tell Brak): 57

F

Fifth International Congress of Orientalists: 28
First World War: interruption of archaeological fieldwork in Mesopotamia, 31
Frankfort, Henri: 96

G

Genesis, Book of: 11, 14, 26, 83
Gihon River: 14, 16, 17
Gilgamesh: 106
Gilgamesh epic: 33, 53, 90, 92; tablets used for, 29
Girsu: 9, 11, 139; terra-cotta head found at, *149*
Gladstone, William: 26
Godin Tepe: 100
Grave goods: 48, 85, *109-117*
Grotefend, Georg Friedrich: and decipherment of Old Persian, 17-18
Gudea: 139, 142, 154, 155, 159; statues of, 27, *118, 137,* 139
Gutians: 128, 137-139, 159

H

Habuba Kabira-Tell Qannas: 57
Halaf culture: 58, 60-61, 65
Halévy, Joseph: 25, 31
Hall, H. R.: excavations at Tell al-Ubaid, 50-51
Hammurabi: code of, 93, 108
Hassuna: 72; alabaster bowl, *60;* alabaster scoop, *60;* excavations at, 61-65
Hebrew: linguistic similarities with Akkadian, 24, 133

Herodotus: 13, 18
Hieroglyphs: 24, 136
Hincks, Edward: decipherment of Akkadian, 23, 24
Huot, Jean-Louis: excavations at Tell Awayli, 68
Hurrians: 128
Hystaspes: 18

I

Ibbi-Sin (king): 144, 145, 146
Illustrated London News: 47, 65
Inanna (deity): 54, 55, 77, 80, 98, 99, 102, 103, 148, 149, 152
Indus Valley: 123
Iran: 128
Iraq: British mandate for, 31-32; independence of, 32, 33, 34
Iraq Antiquities Directorate: 34, 45, 61, 70
Iraqi Antiquities Service: 32
Ishbi-Irra: 145, 146
Ishtar (deity): 148
Isin: 145

J

Jabur tribemen: 61-64
Jarmo: 62; excavations at, 54, *70,* 158; pottery found at, *54*
Jazirah desert: 61
Jebel Aruda: 57; ruins at, *38-39*

K

Karun River: *map* 16, 17
Kaunakes: 26
Keeling, Katharine: 85. *See also* Woolley, Katharine
Khabur River: 60
Khafajah: excavations at, 96-99
Khorsabad: carving found at, *21;* excavations at, 20, 21
Kirkbride, Diana: 72; excavations at Umm Dabaghiyah, 73-74
Kish: 94, 101, 123; excavations at, 101; inlaid plaque found at, *105;* mace head found at, *104;* unification of Sumer, 106, 107
Knudstad, James: 103
Koldeway, Robert: 28, 32
Kramer, Samuel Noah: and Nippur tablets, 104, 105-106
Kurdistan: 124
Kuyunjik mound: 21, 58

L

Lagash: 9, 94, 108, 119, 124, 139, 155, 159; falls to Sargon, 122; rise to power of, 106-107; silver vase found at, *103;* wall plaque from,

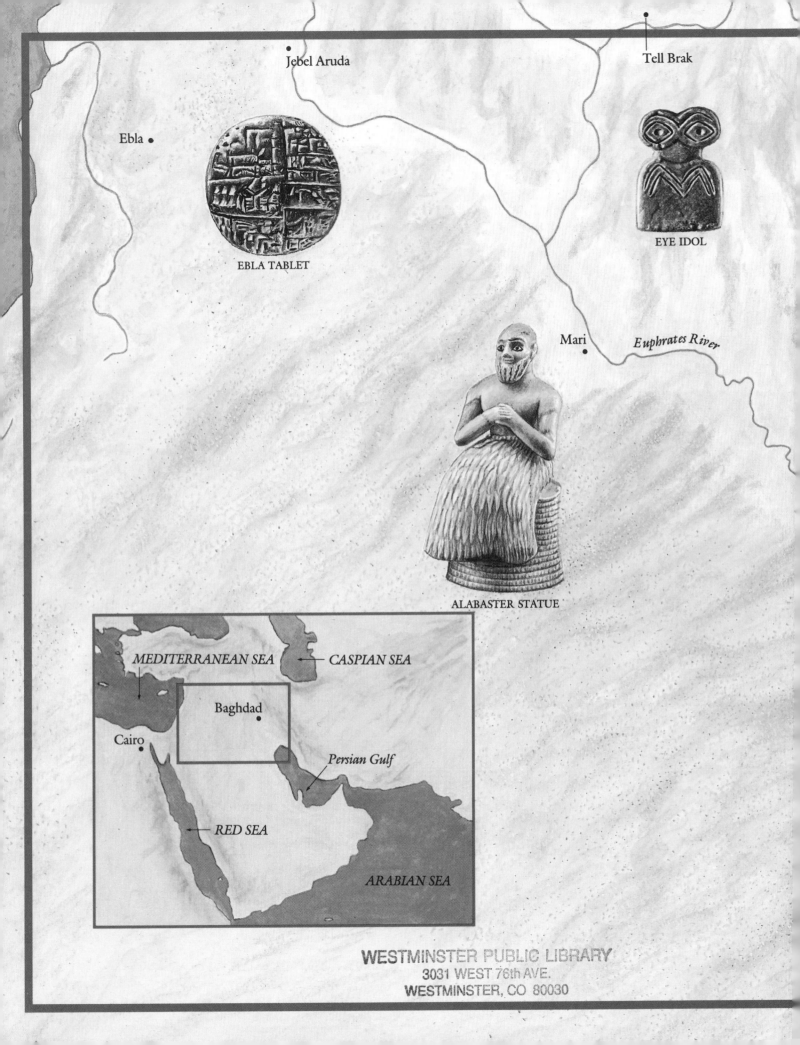

Jebel Aruda

Tell Brak

Ebla

EBLA TABLET

EYE IDOL

Mari   *Euphrates River*

ALABASTER STATUE

MEDITERRANEAN SEA   *CASPIAN SEA*

Baghdad

Cairo

Persian Gulf

RED SEA

ARABIAN SEA